T0323994

Cambridge Elements ≡

Elements in Metaphysics
edited by
Tuomas E. Tahko
University of Bristol

METAPHYSICS OF CAUSATION

Max Kistler
Paris 1 Panthéon-Sorbonne University

CAMBRIDGE
UNIVERSITY PRESS

CAMBRIDGE
UNIVERSITY PRESS

Shaftesbury Road, Cambridge CB2 8EA, United Kingdom

One Liberty Plaza, 20th Floor, New York, NY 10006, USA

477 Williamstown Road, Port Melbourne, VIC 3207, Australia

314–321, 3rd Floor, Plot 3, Splendor Forum, Jasola District Centre,
New Delhi – 110025, India

103 Penang Road, #05–06/07, Visioncrest Commercial, Singapore 238467

Cambridge University Press is part of Cambridge University Press & Assessment,
a department of the University of Cambridge.

We share the University's mission to contribute to society through the pursuit of
education, learning and research at the highest international levels of excellence.

www.cambridge.org
Information on this title: www.cambridge.org/9781009500340

DOI: 10.1017/9781009260800

First published 2024

A catalogue record for this publication is available from the British Library

ISBN 978-1-009-50034-0 Hardback
ISBN 978-1-009-26083-1 Paperback
ISSN 2633-9862 (online)
ISSN 2633-9854 (print)

Cambridge University Press & Assessment has no responsibility for the persistence
or accuracy of URLs for external or third-party internet websites referred to in this
publication and does not guarantee that any content on such websites is, or will
remain, accurate or appropriate.

Metaphysics of Causation

Elements in Metaphysics

DOI: 10.1017/9781009260800
First published online: December 2024

Max Kistler
Paris 1 Panthéon-Sorbonne University
Author for correspondence: Max Kistler, mkistler@univ-paris1.fr

Abstract: This Element presents the main attempts to account for causation as a metaphysical concept, in terms of (1) regularities and laws of nature, (2) conditional probabilities and Bayes nets, (3) necessitation between universals and causal powers, (4) counterfactual dependence, (5) interventions and causal models, and (6) processes and mechanisms. None of these accounts can provide a complete reductive analysis. However, some provide the means to distinguish several useful concepts of causation, such as total cause, contributing cause, direct and indirect cause, and actual cause. Moreover, some of these accounts can be construed so as to complement each other. The last part presents some contemporary debates: on the relation between grounding and causation, eliminativism with respect to causation in physics, the challenge against "downward" causation from the Closure and Exclusion principles, robust and proportional causation, and degrees of causation. This title is also available as Open Access on Cambridge Core.

Keywords: causation, metaphysics, causal models, causal processes, dependence

ISBNs: 9781009500340 (HB), 9781009260831 (PB), 9781009260800 (OC)
ISSNs: 2633-9862 (online), 2633-9854 (print)

Contents

Introduction

Causation is central to our understanding of the world and ourselves. The sciences provide causal explanations. Geology and physics explain the mechanisms that cause earthquakes and the causal processes by which earthquakes cause tsunamis. Biology explains the causes of the appearance of new biological species and of the extinction of other species. Historians explore the causes of antisemitism and the Holocaust. Our understanding of all these cases of causation is itself causally structured, and psychologists study the causal processes of learning, remembering and reasoning. Scientists and philosophers have also practical motivations for improving our understanding of causation. It is after all crucial for improving our means of changing things. Understanding the causes of the increase in economical inequality is inseparable from finding out by what means we might slow it down or reverse it. Understanding the causes of cancer, multiple sclerosis, or Covid-19 is required for conceiving of means for diminishing the incidence of these diseases, for soothing their symptoms and treating them. Understanding causation is also fundamental in the law. Individuals and firms are condemned on the basis of the courts' judgment that they have caused harm. Causation poses a challenge both to philosophy of science and to metaphysics. What do scientists do when they look for and provide causal explanations? The challenge for metaphysics is to understand what reality must be like if causal explanations are true.

Before we look at philosophical theories of causation, we may start with the observation that the concept of causation that is used both in common sense and in science is structured around the following "central connotations of causation" (Schaffer 2000a, p. 289).

1. The causal relation holds between distinct events.[1]
2. The causal relation is intrinsic to these events. In particular, whether a causes b is determined locally, at the spatiotemporal location of a, b and in the region between them. It does not depend on what happens at other times and places.
3. Causes raise the chance of their effects.
4. Causes precede their effects, or at least don't follow them, in time.
5. Asymmetry: if a causes b, it is not the case that b also causes a.
6. Objectivity: whether a causes b does not depend on us or any other observers or explanation-seekers.
7. The cause can be used as a means for making the effect happen.

---

[1] Lewis (1986a). It is often taken for granted that this entails that parts and wholes cannot be causally related, but this has been challenged (Friend 2019).

8. One can infer the effect from knowledge of the cause, and one can infer the cause from knowledge of the effect.
9. Agents are morally and legally responsible for what they cause.
10. Effects depend on their causes. This dependence can be expressed in counterfactuals.

This Element presents the major attempts to account for causation as a metaphysical concept, in terms of (1) regularities and laws of nature, (2) probabilities and Bayes nets, (3) necessitation between universals and causal powers, (4) counterfactual dependence, (5) interventions, (6) causal models, and (7) processes or mechanisms. I will argue that causal models and process accounts are complementary. Causal models provide an account of causation at the level of types, whereas processes account for causation between particular events. The last part presents some contemporary debates in the metaphysics of causation: on the relation between grounding and causation, eliminativism with respect to causation in physics, the challenge against "downward" causation from the Closure and Exclusion principles, robust and proportional causation, and degrees of causation.

1 Regularities and Laws of Nature

David Hume's account of causation is one of the main sources of contemporary attempts to analyze causation in terms of regularity. Hume himself did not offer a metaphysical theory of causation, as it is independently of us, because he was skeptical about the possibility of knowing what it takes, in a metaphysical sense, for one event to cause another.[2] Rather, he offers an epistemological theory of what makes us judge that one event causes another. There are two necessary conditions for a causing b (where a and b are particular events[3]) that Hume claims we can know by observation: that a is earlier than b and that a and b touch each other (in technical jargon, that they are contiguous). Both can be challenged, especially on the background of contemporary physics,[4] but let us leave this to one side here. According to

---

[2] Garrett (2009).

[3] Let us take an event to be something that happens to one or several individuals at a time. Many theses about causation can be expressed both in the language of events and in the language of facts. However, claims about causal relations between facts are often not equivalent to claims about causal relations between events because the meaning of an expression designating an event, such as "the tsunami," is not equivalent to the meaning of a factive expression, such as "the fact that there was a tsunami" (Bennett 1988; Kistler 1999a). We consider the issue of the terms of causal relations in Section 6.1.

[4] On the first requirement: According to the theory of special relativity, judgments of temporal precedence between two events a and b can be relative to a spatiotemporal framework. If two

Hume, the origin of the difference between a causing b and a merely preceding and touching b, is psychological. When we judge that a causes b, rather than just following it, this judgment is based on an expectation that is the result of a psychological process of habituation.

1.1 Regularity Theory

Hume's criteria of contiguity, anteriority and regularity can be used to construct a metaphysical theory of causation.

(R) "c causes e iff

i. c is spatiotemporally contiguous to e;
ii. e succeeds c in time; and
iii. All events of type C (i.e., events that are like c) are regularly followed by (or are constantly conjoined with) events of type E (i.e., events like e)" (Psillos 2009, p. 131).

Interpreting (R) as a metaphysical account of what makes it the case that c causes e excludes interpreting it as, for example, a semantic analysis of the meaning of the term "cause," or as providing an epistemic tool for how the concept of cause can or should be used.[5]

Here are some challenges to (R). It can be doubted (1) that each of conditions (i) – (iii) is individually necessary and (2) that all three are jointly sufficient for it to be the case that c causes e.

1. (i, ii, iii not jointly sufficient for causation) Thomas Reid has famously objected to Hume's theory of causation that it has the absurd consequence

---

observers O and P move relative to one another with high speed (i.e., the speed is non-negligible with respect to the speed of light), and if a and b are spacelike separate (in the sense of the theory of relativity), O may observe that a happens earlier than b, whereas P observes that b happens earlier than a. On the second requirement: If c and d are macroscopic middle-sized objects such as my desk and a book lying on it, I can observe by direct unaided sight that they touch each other. However, it is much less obvious (and controversial, see Russell 1912/1919) whether there is any non-arbitrary criterion for whether these objects touch each other at the level of atoms and molecules. No observational meaning can be given to the application of the notion of touch to atoms or subatomic particles. When, for example, an electron and a photon interact in the process called "Compton scattering," it makes no sense to ask whether they touch each other during this interaction.

[5] Semantics and epistemology are not independent of metaphysics. If (R) were a correct semantic analysis of the meaning of the word "cause" it would also be true as a metaphysical account of causation, yet the reverse does not hold. (R) may be true in the metaphysical sense without being true by virtue of the meaning of the word "cause" alone. Moreover, (R) may be true as a metaphysical account yet it may not always provide a good, or the best, means for our finding out about what causes what, because, for example, information about conditions (i) to (iii) may not always be easily accessible to us. The reverse is also possible: (R) may be a good, or even the best, epistemic tool for our finding out about causation in all situations that are practically relevant for us, although it provides neither a necessary nor a sufficient condition for causation.

that night is the cause of day and day the cause of night.[6] This doesn't seem to be the only case of regular contiguous succession that is not a case of causation.

2. ((ii) not necessary: simultaneous causation) Stable situations seem to contain simultaneous causation: Kant mentions "a ball that lies on a stuffed pillow and makes a dent in it" (Kant 1781/1998, A203/B248, p. 312). Bricks and mortar and their composition cause the stability of a house. In a Newtonian model in which two bodies gravitate around each other only under the influence of the gravitational attraction of their masses, each body's attraction toward the other is, at each instant, caused by their masses at that instant. All of these relations seem to be simultaneous, so that temporal precedence cannot be used to distinguish cause and effect.

3. ((ii) not necessary: backward causation) The possibility of causal influence running in the opposite direction of time, often called "backward causation," is a matter of debate within physics.[7] Therefore, it would be ill-advised to build temporal precedence into the analysis of the concept of causation. This would make backward causation conceptually incoherent. It would mean to construe the concept in a way that is incompatible with its use in science, so that something would come out as conceptually impossible, although science takes it to be possible. Philosophy should construct concepts that are fit for being used in contemporary science.[8]

4. ((iii) not necessary: singular causation) It is probably not correct, from a psychological point of view, that humans (and other animals) learn about causal connections between events only after having observed a succession of events several times. One can learn that flames burn our skin after a single experience of putting our hand in a fire. Moreover, the requirement of regular succession seems difficult to justify from a metaphysical point of view,[9] and it is not clear whether it could be expressed by a formal criterion: If F is a predicate that applies only to a single event a, and if Ga is also true, then Fa and Ga are formally an instance of a regular succession (U) $(x)(Fx \rightarrow Gx)$, though only in a trivial sense.[10]

---

[6] Reid (1788/2010, p. 249). It may be strange to consider night and day to be events because they last quite long. Sunset and sunrise, having shorter duration, make for clearer examples of events that regularly follow each other without one causing the other.

[7] Faye (2024).

[8] Making the temporal precedence of the cause before the effect part of the concept of causation also precludes using the concept of causation in a theory of the direction of time, on pains of circularity (Reichenbach 1928/1958, 1956), Lewis (1973b/1986, p. 170).

[9] It can be denied that singular causation requires regularity. Reid (1788/2010, p. 250); Ducasse (1926, 1966).

[10] Maybe all macroscopic events, and in particular historical events, are unique, and never recur. Cassirer (1910/1923, p. 227n), Russell (1912/1919, p. 187). If this is correct, every succession of

5. ((iii) not necessary: indeterministic causation) Another fundamental problem for regularity theories is that many, and probably most, causal regularities allow for exceptions. Benfluorex causes death by heart failure, although it doesn't do this invariably but only in a significant proportion of cases. Even the most effective drug does not result in recovery in 100% of cases. It is now standard to require of an adequate theory of causation that it be at least adaptable to causal influences that make an effect more probable than it would have been otherwise, without making it certain to occur.[11] C may cause E even if C raises E's probability from 0% only to some very small percentage, such as 0.1%.

1.2 Deductive-Nomological Theory

An influential version of regularity theory has been developed by the philosophers of the school of logical empiricism. As empiricists, they require that scientific facts must be observable at least in principle. Logical empiricism condemns metaphysics as systematically meaningless (Carnap 1931). Nevertheless, the logical empiricist theory of what determines the truth value of causal statements can be interpreted as a metaphysical theory of the causal relations expressed by those statements. "A statement about a causal relation [...] describes an observed regularity of nature, nothing more" (Carnap 1966/1995, p. 201). Carnap's thesis is that the truth value of singular causal statements is determined by the truth value of universal statements expressing regularities. The metaphysical interpretation (not intended by Carnap himself) is a regularity theory of singular causation. The relevant regularities are taken to be (a certain type of) laws of nature.[12] According to this interpretation, whether a causes b is determined by whether there are laws of nature relating type (or description) A, to which a belongs, to type B, to which b belongs. "What is meant when it is said that event B is caused by event A? It is that there are certain laws in nature from which event B can be

---

macroscopic events is an instance of a trivial regularity of the form (U). Carnap's proposal to overcome this problem is mentioned in fn. 17.

[11] See Section 2.

[12] "It is more fruitful to replace the entire discussion of the meaning of causality by an investigation of the various kinds of laws that occur in science. [...] The logical analysis of laws is certainly a clearer, more precise problem than the problem of what causality means" (Carnap 1966/1995, p. 204). We must leave here to one side the debate on what distinguishes laws of nature from (other) regularities. Dretske (1977) and Armstrong (1983) have defended the view that laws are relations of necessitation among universal properties; David Lewis (1973a, 1994) characterizes laws, taking up ideas expressed by Mill and Ramsey, by the role the statements expressing them play in scientific theories. For other accounts, see Maudlin (2007), Lange (2009), Jaag and Schrenk (2020).

logically deduced when they are combined with the full description of event A" (Carnap 1966/1995, p. 194).[13]

According to the so-called Deductive-Nomological (DN) model of scientific explanation[14] (Hempel 1965, p. 247/248), a scientific explanation is a sound argument, that is, a valid deductive argument with true premises. The conclusion of the argument expresses the fact that is up for explanation: the so-called explanandum; the premises of the explanation (the so-called explanans) of a particular fact or event essentially contain (1) a description of particular facts or events, the so-called initial conditions, and (2) at least one law of nature. "Essentially" means that the deductive argument would lose its validity if some part of those premises were omitted. Carnap takes the conditions for the existence of a causal relation to be the same as the conditions for scientific explanation and prediction,[15] so that it is equivalent to say that C causes E and that E can be explained by a valid DN argument on the basis of C.[16]

(DN-C) C causes E if and only if

1. C and E have empirical content and are true,
2. there is a valid argument that has as its premises C and at least one law of nature L, and E as conclusion.
3. Both C and the laws L are indispensable for the validity of the argument.

A useful way to express the link between the DN accounts of explanation and causation is to say that, if we ignore the epistemological aspects of the DN relation between explanans and explanandum and concentrate on the objective facts required to make the explanation correct, we get the metaphysical doctrine according to which causal relations are instances of lawful regularities.

(DN-C) requires the premises to contain laws, that is, regularities that are nomological and not merely accidental. However, defenders of (DN-C) typically identify laws with regularities. "Repetition is all that distinguishes the causal law from a mere coincidence" (Reichenbach 1951, p. 158).[17] If the

---

[13] I will follow the convention of using lower-case letters to represent particular events and upper-case letters to represent statements or propositions describing those events, or types of events.

[14] "Nomological" means "lawful" in the sense of the laws of nature, "nomos" being the Greek word for law.

[15] According to Carnap and Hempel, the logical structure of *prediction* is the same as that of explanation, the difference being epistemic.

[16] Hempel expresses the same equivalence when he says, after introducing the DN account of explanation: "The type of explanation which has been considered here so far is often referred to as causal explanation" (Hempel 1965, p. 250). Later, Hempel changed his mind on this point. In a note added in 1964, he abandons the thesis that all DN explanations are causal, and advances the weaker thesis that "causal explanation is one variety of the deductive type of explanation here under discussion" (Hempel 1965, p. 250, note 6).

[17] Carnap explains that the distinction between regularities that correspond to laws and can be used in the analysis of causation and other, so-called accidental regularities, must be drawn at the level

argument were valid without any laws of nature, but only by virtue of logic, E would follow from C by conceptual or logical necessity. The link between C and E would be tighter than a causal link, which is traditionally thought to be contingent.[18]

Like other theories that take regularities to be constitutive of causal relations between particular events, the DN account of causation conflicts with the intuition that causation is an intrinsic relation.[19] A property P of an object x is intrinsic if and only if the question whether x has P depends only on x itself and not on x's relations to other things. The relation R between x and y is intrinsic if and only if the question whether x and y stand in relation R depends only on x and y, and not on their relations to other things.

The DN account of causation has eventually been abandoned because non-causal dependence can satisfy the conditions for (DN-C). According to (DN-C), the existence of a law (or laws) to the effect that all As are Bs (expressed by the formula $(x)(Ax \rightarrow Bx)$) is *necessary* for an event of type A to cause an event of type B.[20] This has been called the "Principle of the Nomological Character of Causality."[21] However, the reverse implication does not hold. The law that all As are Bs is not *sufficient* to conclude that events of type A cause events of type B. So-called laws of coexistence or association are counterexamples that show that not all DN explanations are causal.[22] Physics has many laws expressing one quantity as a mathematical function of others. The law of the simple pendulum

---

of basic regularity statements. "I define a *basic law* of nature as a statement that has nomic form and is also true" (Carnap 1966/1995, p. 213). To have nomic form (i.e., "lawlike form," Carnap 1966/1995, p. 211), a universal statement must "not speak of any particular position in space or point in time" (Carnap 1966/1995, p. 211). Such statements "are entirely general with respect to space and time; they hold everywhere, at all times. This is characteristic only of *basic* laws. Obviously there are many [...] laws that are not of this kind. [...] For example: 'All the bears in the North Polar region are white'" (Carnap 1966/1995, p. 211). This may solve the problem of singular causation for the regularity theory (Problem 4 in Section 1.1).

[18] DN arguments that are valid without initial conditions do not bear on particular facts; they express reduction relations at the level of laws (Nagel 1961, chap. 11; Tahko 2021). They could not be used to analyze the notion of causation, even on the controversial assumption that the distinction causal / non-causal applied to laws themselves.

[19] The notion of intrinsicness is intuitive but it is difficult to analyze it in a non-circular way. Cf Marshall and Weatherson (2023). We return to this issue in Section 6.1.

[20] Hempel (1965, p. 348).

[21] Davidson (1967/1980, p. 160; 1970/1980, p. 208; 1995). Fodor calls it the "Covering Principle" (Fodor 1989, p. 64). It is controversial whether the entailment guarantees the existence of strict laws (Davidson 1970/1980, p. 208), or whether such laws may be "*ceteris paribus*" and allow for exceptions (Le Pore and Loewer 1987), and whether it guarantees the existence of deterministic laws (Davidson 1970/1980, p. 208) or whether the laws can be probabilistic (Davidson 1995, p. 266).

[22] "Causal explanation is a special type of deductive nomological explanation" (Hempel 1965, p. 148). See Hempel (1965, pp. 348, 352); Salmon (1984, p. 135/6). Many theories of laws of nature contain or imply the opposite thesis that all laws are causal and that every instance of a law corresponds to an instance of causation, for example, Armstrong (1997). See Section 3.

says that the period T of a simple pendulum is proportional to the square root of its length L ($T = 2\pi\sqrt{L/g}$), where g represents the acceleration of massive objects near the surface of the Earth. However, "one surely would not say that that the pendulum's having a period of two seconds was *caused* by the fact that it had a length of 100 centimeters" (Hempel 1965, p. 350). It seems even more obvious that the period of a pendulum is not among the causes of its length.

According to the ideal gas law, expressed by the formula PV=nRT, the product of the pressure (P) and the temperature (T) of an ideal gas is proportional to the volume (V) occupied by the gas, and to the quantity of gas, measured in moles (n), where R represents the ideal gas constant. Given a fixed volume occupied by a gas, maybe the gas's pressure is a cause of its temperature and maybe its temperature is a cause of its pressure, but both are certainly not true at the same time for the same sample.[23]

The law of the simple pendulum and the ideal gas law express mutual functional dependencies between different variables characterizing some physical system at a time. They are "laws of association" or "laws of coexistence," in opposition to laws of succession. In the case of equations expressing the mutual functional dependence between variables, nothing in the law provides any ground for the asymmetry of cause and effect, that is, for taking some of the variables figuring in the equation to correspond to a cause and other variables to correspond to an effect. Furthermore, assuming transitivity, some variables would indirectly cause themselves. If pressure caused temperature and temperature caused pressure, the temperature of a sample of gas at a given moment would indirectly (by way of causing its pressure) cause itself.

Here is another sort of law of association whose instances do not yield instances of causation. The solubility of salt in water is grounded on its molecular structure (NaCl) and on the chemical interactions between sodium (Na^+) and chloride (Cl^-) ions and water molecules. However, the ions composing a given sample of salt do not *cause* the salt's solubility. The dependence of the chemical properties of a macroscopic sample of substance on the properties of its molecular and atomic components is tighter than causal dependence. Tighter still is conceptual dependence. High-density cholesterol is cholesterol, but the high-density cholesterol in someone's blood isn't a cause of the cholesterol in her blood, because the cholesterol is the union of high-density cholesterol and low-density cholesterol.[24]

---

[23] We have seen above several examples of what appears to be "simultaneous causation," some of which are also counterexamples to the DN analysis. However, the cases of simultaneous dependence mentioned here are not clear counterexamples to the analysis in terms of regular succession because they do not appear as causal in the first place.

[24] Spirtes and Scheines (2004).

All this shows that causation cannot be directly reduced to the application of a law to a particular situation. Here is another way of expressing the point. If (DN-C) were interpreted as an implicit definition of "causation," all scientific explanations would be causal. This would result in modifying the sense of the word "causal" so that it becomes equivalent to "scientific." By depriving the concept of causation of its specific content, such a justification of the use of the concept of causation would be only verbal; it would be equivalent to its elimination.

Hempel (1965, p. 352) suggests that a sufficient condition for causation can be obtained by restricting the laws mentioned in (DN-C) to laws of succession: If a (of type A) occurs and there is a law of succession "all As are followed by Bs," then a causes b (of type B). However, this restriction doesn't fill the bill. Depending on how "is followed by" is interpreted, it makes the analysis either tautological or false.

1) If "is followed by" is taken to mean "is followed causally by," the analysis is circular: "If a occurs and there is a law of succession according to which all As are causally followed by Bs then a causes b."

2) If "is followed by" is taken to mean (1) all As are Bs, and (2) if some a is A at t_1, then at some $t_2 > t_1$, there is a b that is B at t_2, then the analysis is refuted by any stable system to which a law of association applies. If a is A at t_1, then if the system is stable (in the sense that the values of variables A and B do not change between t_1 and t_2), then a is A at t_2. If As are Bs by virtue of a law of association, then if a is A at t_2, a is B at t_2. By transitivity, if a is A at t_1, a is B at t_2. However, there is no reason why non-causal dependence and stability together would make for causation.

It remains to be seen whether there is another interpretation of "law of succession" that makes the criterion avoid both circularity and refutation and that could be used in a sufficient condition for causation. Differential equations such as F=ma do not provide a sufficient condition for causation either. In a deterministic framework, the equations of motion that determine future states of a system on the basis of its present state also determine past states of the system on the basis of its present state. Let us call "Galileo's law" the law according to which all massive objects that fall near the surface of the Earth, undergo constant acceleration.[25] From Galileo's law and the speed of a body at

---

[25] It may be doubted that (G) is a law because it mentions the Earth, which is an individual object, rather than containing only qualitative predicates. One may justify that (G) is a law by the fact that it can be derived, in the framework of Newtonian physics, by applying purely qualitative general laws to the Earth. See note 17. (G) is only approximately correct, even if it is specified that the fall happens in a vacuum, but let us neglect this here.

time t, one can determine its speed at both later and earlier times. However, the present state can only be the cause of later states of the system, not of earlier states.

Hempel (1965, p. 353) offers another reason for which the existence of a law does not, together with initial conditions, provide a sufficient condition for causation. Take a beam of light that travels from point A to point B on a path that crosses an interface separating one optical medium from another at some point C; say the beam enters from air into water. Fermat's principle of least time can be used to calculate the position of C, making the time for the light to get from A to B a minimum. (DN-C) yields the wrong result that the light's being at B is among the causes of the beam's crossing the interface at C.

To sum up our critical examination of regularity theories of causation, there is a deep link between causation and lawful regularities but causation cannot simply be reduced to lawful regularity. Regularities are observable *indicators*, or fallible symptoms, of lawful dependencies and causal influences. We learn that flames burn by noticing that burning systematically follows getting too close to a flame. We infer that fluorine causes increased resistance to tooth decay from the existence of a correlation between a high concentration in fluorine in drinking water and lower incidence of tooth decay. The DN theory is an improvement over a simple regularity theory of causation, in that nomological deducibility is a more reliable indicator of causation then mere regular co-occurrence. But from a metaphysical point of view, regularity theories make the mistake of confusing a fallible criterion used as a means for getting knowledge about causation, with causation itself.[26] Causal influence of one factor on another is one thing, and our means for finding out and getting knowledge about that causal influence is something else.

2 Probabilities and Bayes Nets

We have seen that (DN-C) does not provide a sufficient condition for causation: facts that are related by valid nomological deduction are not always causally related. In statistics, great efforts have been deployed to develop an account of the conditions under which causal conclusions can be derived directly from observations (or data) without any use of the controversial notion of a law of nature. The idea is to construct criteria for causal dependence on the basis of conditional probabilities, which are estimated on the basis of the observation

---

[26] Regularity theories of causation "operationalize" causation (Anjum and Mumford 2018, p. 176). Such theories identify a symptom by which we get access to knowledge of causation with causation itself. See Hempel's (1966) criticism of Bridgman's (1927) operationalism.

of relative frequencies.[27] The central hypothesis of statistical analyses of causation is that the fact that the probability of factor B is higher (or lower[28]) in the presence of factor A than in its absence, is a (fallible) indicator of the existence of a causal influence from factor A on factor B.

The attempt of finding statistical methods for discovering relations of causal influence has one big advantage over (DN-C), over and above avoiding the notion of law. It naturally accounts for the fact that causal influence manifests in observable data only statistically, not universally. Smoking causes lung cancer, but not every smoker gets lung cancer, and some nonsmokers do. In complex situations, which are characteristic of all sciences outside fundamental physics, each case is different and a large number of factors contribute positively or negatively to such an eventuality as the development of lung cancer in a particular person. Furthermore, contemporary fundamental physics contains irreducibly probabilistic processes such as radioactive decay, where only a certain percentage of nuclei undergo the process of decomposition. The effect of the radioactive decay of a given particular ^{14}C nucleus, that is, the coming into existence of a ^{14}N nucleus, cannot be deduced by a DN argument from the presence of the ^{14}C nucleus, together with laws. Only its conditional probability can be deduced.

Most proposals for analyzing causation in terms of conditional probabilities do not even attempt to develop an analysis of causation at the level of particular events.[29] Even if it could be established on purely statistical grounds (which is not the case, as we will see), that "smoking causes lung cancer," such a causal influence at the level of populations does not entail that a particular smoker will get lung cancer, or if she gets cancer, that this cancer was caused by her smoking. The causal influence of S on C, at the level of population level factors, is often called "type-level causation," or "causation between types." The relation between type-level causation and causation between particular events falling under these types, or "token-level causation," is controversial. The type-level causal influence of S on C is neither necessary nor sufficient for the token-level fact that person a's smoking causes her to get cancer.

All attempts to analyze causation in terms of conditional probabilities start with the requirement that the cause be correlated with the effect. A necessary condition for S to be a (type-level) cause of C, is that $P(C/S) > P(C)$ or, equivalently,

---

[27] Frequencies provide a means for estimating probabilities, but the two are not equivalent. Gillies (2000, p. 821) suggests that frequentism in the theory of probability commits the mistake of operationalizing probability: it identifies the object of measurement with our epistemic access to it, that is, with our means for measuring it.

[28] A may causally influence B either by increasing B's probability or by lowering it.

[29] Eells (1991) is an exception.

P(C/S)>P(C/non-S). However, correlation is not sufficient for causation. If both lung cancer (C) and cardiovascular disease (D) are due to a common cause, such as smoking (S), then C and D can be correlated although none of C and D has any direct causal influence on the other. Reichenbach (1956, p. 159) has proposed to characterize the concept of common cause in purely probabilistic terms, with the help of the concept of a screening factor. If C and D are correlated so that P(C/D)>P(C/non-D), but if there is no correlation once the probabilities are evaluated conditional on factor S, to that P(C/S&D)=P(C/S&non-D), S is said to "screen off" C from D.[30] This is indeed an indicator of the fact that S is a common cause of C and D, which explains C and D's correlation. However, it is only a fallible indicator, in the sense that the fact that C is a screening factor for A and B is not sufficient for C being a common cause of A and B.[31]

The inference from correlation to causation requires the absence of screening factors. However, it is not possible to obtain a sufficient condition for causation in purely probabilistic terms by using the criterion of the absence of screening factors. Either the absence of screening factors is explicitly expressed as a causal condition or not. In the first case, as in Cartwright's (1979, p. 423) principle: (CC) C causes E iff P(E/C&K)>P(E/K) for all other causes K of E that are not intermediate between C and E, we don't have an analysis of causation in terms of probabilities alone because the analysans contains information about causes.

In the second case, the requirement that there are no screening factors is expressed in purely probabilistic terms. This doesn't provide an appropriate analysis of causation either, for the following reasons. (1) It yields a requirement that is empirically unrealistic: conditionalizing on all other factors means comparing populations that are homogeneous with respect to all other factors.[32] Such populations do not exist outside of fundamental physics. (2) If we could somehow observe homogenous populations (homogenous except for the factors C and E), we wouldn't find probabilities different from 0 and 1 except if

---

[30] Reichenbach (1956, p. 159) attempts to analyze both the direction of causation and the direction of time in terms of such screening factors. Realism with respect to causation can be combined with perspectivalism about its direction. The direction of a causal link may be determined by the perspective of some observer and/or intervener on the system under study (Price and Weslake 2009).

[31] If C is intermediate between A and B (A causes C, which causes B), then C screens off A from B but it not a common cause of A and B. Salmon (1980, p. 59) gives another example, due du E. Crasnow, of a situation where A, B and C satisfy Reichenbach's conditions for C screening off A and B from each other, but where C is not a common cause of A and B. In the example, a fourth variable D is the common cause of all three, A, B, and C.

[32] "Homogenous with respect to all other factors" means that for each variable representing one of the other factors, that variable has the same value for all individuals within the population.

factors C and E belong to fundamental physics.[33] Intermediate probabilities (e.g., in medicine or social sciences) stem from the fact that empirically accessible populations are not homogeneous.

Now, here is the main problem we face in all situations where frequencies are measured in populations that are not homogeneous: as long as conditional probabilities are estimated from the observation of non-homogeneous populations, in other words, as long as not all factors different from C and E are held fixed, measures of conditional probabilities are always provisional. Judgments of comparative conditional probability are always at risk of being reversed once new factors are taken into account. Such reversal of conditional probabilities is known as Simpson's reversal or Simpson's paradox. Here is an example.[34] A study on thyroid disease found that the survival rate over twenty years (L) of smokers (S) was higher than that of non-smokers. However, it would be mistaken to conclude from P(L/S)>P(L/non-S) that smoking is a causal factor increasing the chance of survival. Age turns out to be a so-called confounding factor. Once frequencies are calculated conditional on age, the inequality is reversed: In six out of seven age groups, the rate of survival was lower for smokers than for non-smokers, and the difference was minimal in the seventh.

This means that we can safely judge whether the higher conditional probability of E given C than given not-C is due to the causal influence of C on E, only if we know all confounding factors. However, confounding factors are typically common causes of C and E. In other words, it is possible to extract information about causal influence from information about conditional probabilities only on the basis of causal knowledge. This is often expressed by the slogan "no causes in, no causes out."[35]

The development of Bayesian networks from the 1980s has much improved statistical methods for discovering (type-level) causal relations between variables. Bayes nets provide powerful means for estimating conditional probabilities on the basis of other probabilities. A Bayes net is a model, which can be represented as a graph that consists of (1) nodes, occupied by variables representing features of target systems, (2) directed edges linking some of these nodes to others, and (3) a probability distribution of each variable conditional on its "parents" in the graph. The set of parents of a variable A is the set of variables that are at the origin of an edge pointing toward A. Bayes nets are constructed on the basis of that probability distribution, together with a fundamental assumption, the "Markov condition." The Markov condition says that each variable is probabilistically independent of its non-descendants, conditional on its parents

---

[33] Fitelson and Hitchcock (2011, p. 601).

[34] Appleton, French, and Vanderpump (1996), Pearl and Mackenzie (2018, p. 210).

[35] Cartwright (1989, chap. 2), Pearl (2000, xiii), Pearl and Mackenzie (2018).

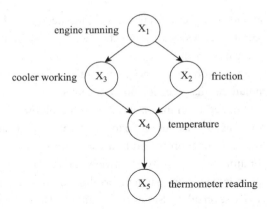

Figure 1 A Bayesian network representing dependencies among five variables. The running of the engine (X_1) causes both friction (X_2) and the working of the cooler (X_3). Both friction and the working of the cooler influence the temperature (X_4) of the engine, which influences the reading of the thermometer (X_5).

in the graph. In other words, all correlations between variables that are not related as cause and effect are due to parent variables, and disappear once the probabilities are calculated conditional on these parent variables. Bayes nets are required to be acyclic, in the sense that they must not contain any circular path, where a path is a sequence of adjacent edges whose directions are aligned.

Here is an example.[36]

In Figure 1, variable X_5 has, for example, only parent variable, X_4. By construction of the net, the probability of X_5, given X_4, is independent of all other variables, that is, X_1, X_2, and X_3.

Although the links in a Bayes net are oriented (from parents to descendants or "children"), they become causal only by virtue of an interpretation. A Bayes net becomes a causal net by interpreting the arrows as representing direct causal influence between variables. In such a causal interpretation, the Markov condition becomes the causal Markov condition, according to which every variable in the net is probabilistically independent of its non-effects, conditional on its direct causes.[37] If a causal net is interpreted as representing a certain system or type of systems, one can read off from that causal net the relations of causal influence between variables. Whether the results are correct of some real system depends on several hypotheses: that the set of variables V represents all causally relevant factors, that the probability distribution P over these variables represents the physical probabilities of the factors represented by these variables, and

---

[36] It shares the structure of Pearl's (2000, p. 15) example.   [37] Hitchcock (2009, p. 306/7).

that the causal net represents the smallest directed acyclic graph on V that satisfies the Markov condition with respect to P.

From a metaphysical point of view, what we want to know is whether causal nets are a reliable tool in the sense of representing relations of causal influence in reality. First, causal nets have been introduced as tools for discovering and representing causal influence between general factors, which provides no direct information about causation between particular events.[38] Second, powerful as they are, they constitute a tool that is as fallible as the hypotheses that are presupposed by their construction.

The Causal Markov Condition implies the following version of Reichenbach's Principle of the Common Cause (Williamson 2009, p. 200):

(PCC) If variables A and B are probabilistically dependent then one causes the other or there is a set U of common causes in V which screens off A and B, that is, renders them probabilistically independent.

There seem to be many systems for which PCC is not correct because they contain factors that stand in non-causal dependence relations. Such dependence can be the consequence of logical, mathematical, or semantical constraints or of non-causal association laws; correlations may also exist in the absence of any common causes and any other constraint (Sober 2001). Variables representing aspects of physical systems that are non-causally related can be probabilistically correlated although neither is a cause of the other and there is no characteristic that plays the role of a common cause so that it could be represented by a variable that screens them off from each other.[39]

Examples may be found in quantum theory. It has been argued that EPR experiments in quantum mechanics give rise to correlations between the states of entangled particles that are not screened off by common causes yet cannot be causal either.[40] However, we can sidestep the controversial interpretation of quantum correlations. Here is Cartwright's (2007, p. 122) example of non-causally correlated variables whose correlation is not screened off by any common causes. Z is a chemical reaction that produces substance X and as a by-product substance Y. The probability of getting X (the value[41] of variable X is 1; in short X=1) from Z (Z=1) is 0.8. We get Y (Y=1) if and only if we get X (X=1). Z is the common cause of X and Y. X and Y are correlated, yet the correlation

---

[38] Causal models can be used to represent so-called "actual" causation, which is intended to correspond to causation between particular events. See Hitchcock (2009, p. 310–3), and Sections 5 and 6.1.

[39] Schurz (2017), Gebharter and Retzlaff (2020).

[40] Hausman (1998, p. 251/2), Healey (2009).

[41] This is an example of actual causation, where cause and effect are represented by values of variables, not variables.

does not vanish upon conditionalizing on the common cause (Z=1). P(X=1/Y=1&Z=1)=1> P(X=1 / Z=1)=0.8.

In Cartwright's example, X=1 is not a cause of Y=1 although the variables X and Y are probabilistically correlated and although their correlation is not screened off by their common cause Z. Such examples show that probabilistic correlation that persists, once the probabilities are calculated conditional on common causes, is not sufficient for causation.

However, it would be a mistake to conclude that they refute the Causal Markov Condition (CMC). The CMC is a condition that holds by convention, in the sense that it is an assumption that is used to construct causal nets.[42] What Cartwright's case shows is that the assumptions built into causal nets, and the CMC in particular, make it problematic to draw realistic conclusions on the causal influence relations in real systems, from causal nets built on the basis of those assumptions. In other words, if Cartwright is correct, then our conventions may prohibit us from constructing a causal net which models the world's actual causal structure.

Maybe a model such as Cartwright's, containing only variables X, Y, and Z, which does not satisfy the CMC, could in principle be completed (Pearl 2000, p. 62) by the addition of some hitherto unknown and unobserved variable intermediate between Z, X, and Y, to yield a model that satisfies CMC. However, there is no guarantee that one can always find such variables that can be interpreted as representing features of the real systems that are the target of the model.

A similar reply is that one should avoid choosing variables that are non-causally related.[43] The PCC holds of all models that are constructed without such variables. However, such a rule would undermine the prospect of using causal nets for the search for causal relations in real systems. For it would mean that we could use the PCC as a criterion for causal relations in real systems only if we knew beforehand (1) which variables to include in the model because they might be causes of the variables whose causes we are looking for and (2) which dependence relations are causal and which are not. If we have that knowledge before we even start building our models, we can build models using only causally related variables (satisfying the CMC). Statistical correlation without any common cause represented in the model can then be used as a sufficient condition for causation in the systems represented by the model.[44]

---

[42] Pearl (2000, p. 62), Hitchcock (2021). "There cannot be counterexamples to CMC, simply because assuming CMC to hold does not imply any empirical consequences" (Gebharter 2017, p. 32).

[43] Woodward (2008), Weslake (forthcoming).

[44] For a similar point, see Williamson (2009, p. 200).

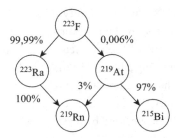

Figure 2 Cascade of radioactive decomposition of ^{223}Fr.

The hypothesis that probabilistic correlation is a *necessary* condition for causation is problematic too. Some real systems contain causal influence relations that are not reflected in the corresponding conditional probabilities. We will look at an example illustrating this in a moment. First note that although, in general, positive causal influence of factor C on factor E increases the probability of E, given C, that is, P(E/C)>P(E/not-C), and negative causal influence of C on E manifests as P(E/C)<P(E/not-C), this is not always the case. Take the radioactive decay of nuclei of the isotope ^{223}Fr of Francium,[45] represented in Figure 2.[46]

99.994% of ^{223}Fr decay into ^{223}Ra, whereas the rest (0.006%) decays into ^{219}At. Both ^{223}Ra nuclei and 3% of ^{219}At nuclei then decay into ^{219}Rn. Take a nucleus of ^{219}At which is at the causal origin of a nucleus of ^{219}Rn. It is much less likely to obtain a ^{219}Rn, given a ^{219}At nucleus, than it would have been if it had been a ^{223}Ra nucleus. After all, only a small portion of ^{219}At become ^{219}Rn (97% of ^{219}At become ^{215}Bi), whereas all ^{223}Ra become ^{219}Rn. This is a case where ^{219}At has a positive causal influence on ^{219}Rn, in the sense that the former nucleus is the causal source of the latter. However, this positive causal influence is not reflected in a higher probability of the effect given the cause, so that probability raising is not necessary for positive causal influence: The probability of having an effect of type ^{219}Rn is lower given the cause (a nucleus of type ^{219}At) than given the alternative possibility that the nucleus be of type ^{223}Ra.[47]

---

[45] Francium has been discovered by French physicist Marguerite Perey in 1939.
    www.lnhb.fr/nuclides/Fr-223_com.pdf
    www.lnhb.fr/nuclides/At-219_tables.pdf
    www.lnhb.fr/nuclides/Ra-223_tables.pdf.

[46] Dowe (1993) offers another example. The structure of the relevant situations is analyzed in Salmon (1984, p. 200/1), Dowe (2000, p. 34), Williamson (2005, 114/5, 2009, p. 201), Kutach (2014, p. 48).

[47] The probability of the effect given the cause depends on the contrast (Hitchcock 1996). A cause may lower the probability of its effect given one contrast and yet raise it given another contrast. In our example, P(^{219}Rn/^{219}At)<P(^{219}Rn/^{223}Ra), but we can easily find a contrast with respect to

It is neither necessary that the probability of the effect is higher given the cause (as we have just seen) nor that it is lower given the cause. Some causes are probabilistically independent of their effects. Take a roulette wheel without a "0." B is the event of throwing a ball in the roulette; B takes value b_0 if the ball had fallen on black after the preceding throw; B takes value b_1 if it had fallen on red after the preceding throw; variable C takes value c if the ball falls on a pair number. Within a framework specified by these variables, B is the only possible cause of C=c, with $P(c/b_0)=P(c/b_1)=1/2$. Here B is a cause of C but B and C are probabilistically independent.[48]

Moreover, many (and probably most) causal interactions at the level of particular events are conceived by concepts which do not give rise to any correlations. Here is Dowe's example: "Two men collide in the corridor. One gets a bruise on his arm, the other drops his papers. [. . .] No one would expect to find any useful statistical correlations between bruises and sets of disordered papers" (Dowe 1992, p. 206).[49]

Causal influence relations between variables do not always manifest in the form of the raising or lowering of the probability of the effect, conditional on the cause. Is this an obstacle to the use of causal nets to represent causal relations in real systems? The situation is similar to the problem raised by non-causal relations that refute the PCC. Causal influence without probability raising is excluded from causal nets by stipulation, by means of the so-called Causal Faithfulness Condition (CFC). A model satisfies the CFC if and only if every conditional independence relation true in the probability distribution P corresponding to the graph (V,E), where V is a set of variables V and E a set of edges, is entailed by the CMC (Spirtes et al. 2000, p. 31).

The CFC is another condition that is, in addition to the Causal Markov condition, stipulated as part of the standard algorithm for the construction of

---

which ^{219}At raises the probability of ^{219}Rn, for example, $P(^{219}Rn/^{219}At)>P(^{219}Rn/^{12}C)$, that is, the probability of finding a ^{219}Rn nucleus given a ^{12}C nucleus, which cannot decay into ^{219}Rn.

    There seem to be two possibilities. Either the criterion is taken to express the condition that it is necessary that the probability of the effect is greater in the presence of the cause than in the presence of some arbitrary contrast. This condition is trivially satisfied, for it would seem that there is always some contrast for which this is the case. Or the criterion is taken to mean that that it is necessary that the probability of the effect is greater in the presence of the cause than in the presence of some contrast that is relevant in the context. In this interpretation, our example shows that it is not plausible that it is a necessary condition for causation. In the context sketched in Figure 2, where the decay cascade starts with ^{223}Fr, the only relevant contrast for ^{219}At is ^{223}Ra, and there is no relevant contrast with respect to which the presence of a ^{219}At nucleus raises the probability of the presence of a ^{219}Rn nucleus.

[48] Williamson (2009, p. 201) makes this point with a schematic example.

[49] Salmon has given up characterizing causal interactions in terms of statistical correlations, for related reasons. Salmon (1984, p. 174, note 12); (1994/1998, p. 251/2). This is related to the point made above (note 10) that most events are unique in the sense of being the unique members of the extension of many concepts.

causal nets from data on probability distributions over a set of variables. The Causal Markov condition roughly says that all statistical correlations between variables X and Y are either due to the fact that X causally influences Y or to the fact that X and Y have common causes. The Causal Faithfulness Condition roughly says that, if variables X and Y are probabilistically independent, neither causally influences the other and they do not have common causes. The Faithfulness condition rules out the possibility, among others,[50] that X causally influences Y through two different paths whose effects exactly cancel each other out, in such a way that the total effect of X on Y is null. It is controversial whether this can happen in real systems. On one hand, external perturbations (i.e., noise) that influence each variable independently of the others make violations of the CFC by exact cancelation very improbable.[51] On the other hand, given that the values of the variables characterizing real systems can be measured only with finite precision, the cancelation of *measured* values seems possible. Indeed, many biological and artificial systems possess features that are designed to remain stable under external influences.[52] Let T represent the temperature of an animal's body, H the heat in the environment, and C the state of a cooling mechanism. If C works well, the causal influences of H and C on T will cancel out, so that T remains stable under variations of H. If the values of these variables are discrete and correspond to measures with finite precision, it may well be that the cancelation is exact, so that H and T are not correlated.[53]

Let me conclude this section on the link between probability raising and causation with the following case.[54] Consider an atom that has a very low probability, say .01, of decaying during a given time interval. The atom is hit by a neutron, which raises its probability of decaying in that interval to .99. The probabilities can be interpreted both as epistemic and, by the lights of contemporary physics, as physical chances independent of our knowledge. The collision of the atom with the neutron raises its probability of decaying although the collision is neither necessary nor sufficient for its decaying. The probabilities alone provide no reason why the fact that the collision raises the probability of the decay should entail that it causes the decay. True, the collision made the decay more probable, yet nothing precludes the possibility that the decay was exclusively due to factors internal to the atom, and thus that the collision was not the cause of the decay.

---

[50] Gebharter (2017, p. 34/5).   [51] Spirtes et al. (2000, p. 41/2), Gebharter (2017, p. 37).

[52] Cartwright (1999, p. 118), Andersen (2013).

[53] Schurz (2017) suggests modifying the algorithm for the construction of causal nets so that violation of both the Causal Markov Condition and the Causal Faithfulness Condition in real systems can be taken into account.

[54] Hitchcock (2003, p. 17, 2004).

The fact that one factor A raises the probability of a second factor B, independently of the background as in the case just considered, or against the background of a causal net, is a strong but fallible indicator of the fact that A causally influences B. It is fallible indicator in the sense that A may not have any causal influence on B, although A raises B's probability, and A may causally influence B although this isn't manifest in the probabilities.

3 Necessitation between Universals and Causal Powers

If regularities and statistical correlation are only fallible indicators of causation, what is causation itself? Let us look at attempts to analyze causation with the help of specifically metaphysical concepts, such as necessitation between universals and causal powers.[55]

David Armstrong analyses singular causation in terms of the instantiation of structural universals.[56] Every case of causation results from the instantiation of a causal law; and a causal law is a relation of necessitation of one universal by another. "The fundamental causal relation is a nomic one, holding between state-of-affairs types, between universals. Singular causation is no more than the instantiation of this type of relation in particular cases" (Armstrong 1997, p. 227). Armstrong gives the example of "guillotining (that state-of-affairs type) causing immediate decapitation (a further state-of-affairs type). It is a second order state of affairs, a relation holding between the universals involved. This second order state of affairs must itself be a universal, a structural universal involving a certain linking of universals, a linking of state-of-affairs-types" (Armstrong 1997, p. 226/7).

The postulate of universals is a controversial metaphysical hypothesis, which we cannot evaluate here. Let me mention three difficulties that stand in the way of the possibility of explaining causation in terms of universals. (1) Even if universals are accepted, the postulate of a second order universal of causal

---

[55] Necessitation between universals and causal powers are entities postulated by metaphysicians. Woodward (2015a) (see also Woodward 2014, 2021a) argues that the postulate of such specifically metaphysical entities belongs to a theoretical enterprise, ontology$_2$/metaphysics$_2$, that differs from what he calls ontology$_1$, which consists in extracting commitment to what exists from successful scientific theories and models. It is controversial whether this distinction is as sharp as Woodward claims or whether it is just a difference in level of abstraction. The present section is the only one in this Element that belongs to ontology$_2$/metaphysics$_2$ in Woodward's sense.

[56] The concept of structure relevant here is different from the concept relevant for "structural equations," presented in Section 5. The latter makes use of a mathematical structure of functional dependence, whereas Armstrong uses a metaphysical concept of dependence among universals. Being a hydrogen atom is a structural universal that is instantiated in a particular object by virtue of the fact that the object has parts standing in a specific relation, one of which instantiates the universal of being a proton and the other the universal of being an electron (Armstrong 1978, p. 70).

necessitation relating one universal (guillotining) to another (decapitating) raises the worry that Armstrong's theory explains something familiar, that is, causation between states of affairs, in terms of something that is much more mysterious than what it is supposed to explain. If we don't know what causation is at the level of singular events or states of affairs, does it help to learn that it is the instantiation of a causal relation between universals? (2) The "instantiation" of causation between universals by causation between instances of those universals raises what van Fraassen has called the "inference problem" (Lewis 1983, p. 366; van Fraassen 1989, p. 96). How can laws, as relations between universals, explain regularities at the level of singular instances of these universals? (3) Armstrong's theory also suffers from a more specific problem that it shares with the DN account: given that it takes all laws to be causal, it cannot account for non-causal association laws.

Others have suggested explaining causation in terms of the manifestation of causal powers (Bird 2010; Mumford and Anjum 2010, 2011). The metaphysical theory of causal powers (Ellis 2001; Molnar 2003) challenges the assumption that events are metaphysically independent of one another, and that causation is an external relation between them. Rather, causation is built into the natural properties constituting events. These properties are causal powers that are, by their very nature, disposed to manifest in specific ways, according to the circumstances. According to the power theory of causation, the relation between cause and effect can be analyzed in terms of the relation between a power and its manifestation. Given that powers are causal by definition, such an analysis is not reductive. Mumford and Anjum's version of this theory makes several original and controversial claims. Causes do not necessitate their effects, in the sense of being sufficient conditions for them, although they necessarily give rise to a tendency toward their effects. This tendency is a sui generis form of modality, irreducible to contingency and necessity (Anjum and Mumford 2018a). Causes and effects are always simultaneous, and causation is non-symmetric and non-transitive (Mumford and Anjum 2011). The combined action of several powers can be represented in terms of the addition of vectors. Causation can be directly perceived, in particular in proprioception. I can do justice here neither to the metaphysics of powers nor to these specific theses about causation. However, it can be challenged whether it is possible to account for causation that extends over time, on the basis of the thesis that all causation is simultaneous (Chakravartty 2013; McKitrick 2013). It can also be challenged whether the analogy between the combination of causes and vector addition is satisfactory, given that causes often interact, in the sense that the effect of several causes acting together is not simply the cumulative result of the addition of the effects of each of them taken individually (Fenton-Glynn 2012; Chakravartty 2013).

4 Counterfactual Dependence

Some correlations do not correspond to any causal influence (and some cases of causal influence do not manifest in correlations). What distinguishes those correlations that are grounded on causal influence from those that are not?

David Hume developed the first regularity theory of causation. However, in one of his definitions he characterizes the relation between cause and effect in counterfactual form. "We may define a cause to be *an object, followed by another, and where all the objects similar to the first are followed by objects similar to the second. Or in other words where, if the first object had not been, the second never had existed*" (Hume 1777/1975, p. 76, italics in original). David Lewis (1973b/1986) and others[57] have developed this counterfactual condition, which Hume presents as an alternative but equivalent formulation of the regularity theory, into a new theory of causation. Counterfactual theories of causation are motivated by the strong intuitive link between causation and certain counterfactual statements. Event c is a cause of event e if and only if c makes some difference to e, and difference-making can be expressed in counterfactual form: If c had not occurred, e would not have occurred.[58]

The counterfactual approach to causation between particular events takes causation to be equivalent to a certain form of dependence. True, causation is a form of dependence. However, not every dependence is causal. Counterfactual theories of causation have attempted to find appropriate additional constraints on dependence in order to obtain a sufficient condition for causation. These constraints result from a reflection on cases of dependence that seem clearly non-causal; the aim is to construct an account that avoids those counterexamples.

One constraint on cause and effect is that they are distinct particular events in the sense that they do not share any part. This allows for avoiding the result that the following cases of (counterfactual) dependence be wrongly considered as causal, which they are not. If I had not spoken this sentence, I would not have spoken the first half of it.[59] The events of my speaking this sentence and of my speaking the first half of it are not distinct because the second is a part of the first. Without the constraint according to which cause and effect must be distinct events, this would be a "false positive," a counterexample, which the counterfactual theory of causation wrongly categorizes as causal.

---

[57] Menzies and Beebee (2024), Noordhof (2020).

[58] Several authors (Lewis 1986, p. 176/7; Menzies 1996) have developed probabilistic versions of the counterfactual account. Instead of requiring that event e counterfactually depends on event c, it is required that "e probabilistically depends on c," which means that "if c were to occur, the chance of e's occurring would be x, and if c were not to occur, the chance of e's occurring would be y, where x is much greater than y" (Menzies 1996, p. 87).

[59] Lewis (1986a, p. 259).

Other constraints have been introduced to avoid that later events be wrongly considered as causes of earlier events although there seem to be many cases of so-called "backtracking" counterfactual dependence.

(1) Let us suppose that there are situations in which e_1 causes e_2 in such a way that the occurrence of e_1 is a sufficient condition for the occurrence of e_2. Nothing could prevent e_2 once e_1 has happened. A plausible case may be two successive events e_1 and e_2 on the trajectory of a particle traveling in a straight line through empty space. If e_1 is a sufficient condition for e_2, e_2 is a necessary condition for e_1: if e_2 hadn't happened, that can only be because e_1 has not happened. So it would seem that the backtracking counterfactual $\neg e_2 \rightarrow \neg e_1$ is true. Without additional constraints, this is a counterexample that refutes the analysis because e_2 is not a cause of e_1.

(2) Cases of counterfactual dependence between so-called epiphenomena are another source of counterexamples. If c is a common cause of e_1 and e_2, then there can be counterfactual dependence of one effect, e_2, on the other e_1. Let c represent a drop in atmospheric pressure, e_1 a drop in my barometer's reading, and e_2 a storm. If c is a sufficient condition for e_1 and c is a necessary condition of e_2, then $\neg e_1 \rightarrow \neg c$ and $\neg c \rightarrow \neg e_2$, and it may also be the case (though there is no valid inference to this effect) that $\neg e1 \rightarrow \neg e_2$. The storm may be counterfactually dependent on the fall of the barometer but it is not caused by it.

Both problems can be solved if backtracking counterfactuals are excluded. This requirement may be added as an additional constraint, or it may be argued that it results from the semantics of counterfactuals, that is, that it is implicit in the meaning of counterfactual statements.[60]

Additional constraints are also required to yield a form of counterfactual dependence that is necessary for causation. Without such constraints, there are

---

[60] Lewis argues that backtracking counterfactuals come in general out false on the basis of the semantics that is implicit in our intuitive evaluation of counterfactuals. According to the semantic rules that Lewis' (1973a) theory of counterfactuals makes explicit, we take the counterfactual to be true if the consequent is true in the closest possible world in which the antecedent is true. On the basis of the criteria we use (which Lewis also makes explicit), the closest world to our actual world in which the counterfactual antecedent is true is always a world in which a "tiny miracle" (1979/1986, p. 44) occurs just before the occurrence of the antecedent. It is controversial whether it is enough to argue that, according to our general strategy for the evaluation of counterfactuals, the antecedent is always taken to be the result of a miracle, to get the result that backtracking counterfactuals are systematically false (Elga 2001). Even if Lewis' thesis is accepted that the miracles we consider in our procedure for the evaluation of counterfactuals are located in the past of the antecedent, it might be argued that the miracle must lie outside the interval between antecedent and consequent. In case of a backwards counterfactual, the relevant miracle would be situated immediately before the consequent, so that backwards counterfactuals could be judged true.

cases of causation where the effect does not counterfactually depend on its cause. These are "false negatives," that is, counterexamples that the counterfactual theory of causation wrongly categorizes as not causal.

If a cause is accompanied by a backup event, the effect is not counterfactually dependent on the cause, for the effect would have occurred in the absence of the cause, thanks to the presence of the backup. Redundant causation corresponds to situations where both events are effective in bringing out the effect. In situations where the backup cause is not effective, the effective cause is said to "preempt" the backup cause. The backup cause has the potential to cause the effect in the absence of the effective, preemptive cause. There is counterfactual dependence of the effect on the cause neither in cases of redundant causation nor in cases of preemption. Redundant and backup causes are widespread in biology. If the causal role of some organ A is vital, organisms will have higher fitness if they have a redundant or backup organ B that takes over whenever A is not well functioning. Each of our kidneys is redundant given the presence and functioning of the other. Here is a biological example of preemption.[61] Even in a healthy brain, neurons die at a certain rate, which increases with age. As dead cells and cellular debris accumulate, they harm surrounding cells, which in turn accelerates neuron death and causes neurodegenerative diseases such as Alzheimer's disease. Microglia are cells that remove cellular debris from the brain. However, if microglia fail to accomplish their function, astrocytes, another kind of brain cell, step in to remove debris as a backup to microglia.

Cases of redundant causes and preemption point to a deep problem with all counterfactual theories. According to counterfactual theories, whether c causes e depends not only on c, e, and what happens in the spatiotemporal region between these events, but also on what goes on elsewhere. This contradicts the intuition that causation is intrinsic to the relata and the region between them.[62]

Lewis (1973b/1986) has adapted the counterfactual analysis to this type of situation by requiring that there exist a series of intermediate events between the cause and effect so that each of the events in the series is counterfactually dependent on its predecessor. In cases of so-called "early preemption," there is indeed no stepwise counterfactual dependence of the effect on the preempted (i.e., non-effective) backup cause. However, this solution raises the problem

---

[61] Konishi et al. (2020).

[62] See Section 6.1. Lewis has suggested to solve the problem of (late) preemption with the help of the concept of "quasi-dependence" (Lewis 1986, p. 206), with the result that causation is construed as an intrinsic relation, that is, in a way that makes c's causing e independent of c's and e's relations to other events.

that it builds transitivity into the concept of causation. It is controversial whether transitivity is part of the concept of causation.[63]

Anyway, the requirement of the existence of an intermediate chain with stepwise counterfactual dependence cannot account for some types of preemption, in particular "late pre-emption" and "trumping pre-emption" (Schaffer 2000/2004),[64] which corresponds to the overdetermination of an event by two independent causes. To take Schaffer's example of trumping preemption, if both the Major and the Sergeant give the Corporal at the same time the same order, for example, the order to advance, the behavior of the Corporal is overdetermined, in the sense that it is caused twice over. Given that the Major's rank is higher, it is plausible that his order is the cause of the Corporal's moving, but this effect does not counterfactually depend on its cause.

The counterfactual approach has mostly been interpreted by its advocates as belonging to conceptual analysis. The intuition that our concept of causation has at least a strong counterfactual component provides enough motivation to develop the account so as to cope with counterexamples. It is indeed plausible that the semantics of causal statements can be analyzed in terms of counterfactuals, whose truth conditions can in turn be analyzed in the framework of possible worlds. The psychological mechanisms of reasoning about causation also seem to involve reasoning about counterfactual situations.[65] However, the role of counterfactuals for metaphysics is more controversial. Other possible worlds can be interpreted not only as a semantic tool but also as what makes true counterfactual statements in a metaphysical sense.[66] Alternatively, the truth-makers[67] of counterfactuals may be taken to be part of the actual world: either laws of nature, or powers or potentialities.[68]

5 Interventions and Causal Models

A strong motivation for searching knowledge about causation is that such knowledge enables us to control things. If I know that A causes B I can exploit that knowledge to obtain B by manipulating A. The same connection allows us,

---

[63] Many authors argue that transitivity is not part of the concept of causation (McDermott 1995; Hitchcock 2001, 2003; Noordhof 2020).

[64] Lewis has attempted to solve the problem raised by trumping preemption by the requirement that a cause must "influence" its effect (Lewis 2000/2004), but without success (Kvart 2001). Lewis' theory of causation as influence may be inspired by Reichenbach who writes: "If E_1 is the cause of E_2, then a small variation (a mark) in E_1 is associated with a small variation in E_2." Reichenbach seems to presuppose that the former "variation" is brought about by an intervention, which provides an account of the asymmetry of causation and the distinction between the cause and the effect: "whereas small variations in E_2 are not associated with variations in E_1" (Reichenbach 1928/1958, §21, p. 136).

[65] Kahneman and Tversky (1982), Quillien (2020).   [66] Lewis (1986b).

[67] Armstrong (2004).   [68] Borghini and Williams (2008), Vetter (2015).

in the other direction, to obtain causal knowledge by manipulation. Observing the effects of our own manipulations plays an important role in the psychological mechanisms that allow humans to acquire causal knowledge (Gopnik and Schulz 2007; Waldmann 2017). In experimental sciences, interventions are a crucial method for discovering causal influences, in addition to the observation of correlations. Under certain conditions (to which we return shortly), if an experimenter manipulates a variable C and observes a subsequent variation in variable E, this indicates that C causally influences E.

Structural equations (SE), a formal tool first introduced in genetics (Wright 1921) and econometrics (Haavelmo 1943), can be used to build models of causal structures on the basis of information obtained in this way, completing the models built in the framework of Bayes nets.[69] The philosophical analysis of such causal models integrates insights of older philosophical theories of causation in terms of manipulation by a free agent, according to which "an event A is a cause of a distinct event B just in case bringing about the occurrence of A would be an effective means by which a free agent could bring about the occurrence of B."[70] However, in that form, such an account suffered from two major defects: circularity and anthropocentrism. The latter is implicit in the thesis that an event can be a cause only if its occurrence can be the result of the decision of a free agent.[71] We will see shortly that recent accounts in terms of causal models replace the concept of manipulation by the concept of intervention, which is not tied to free action, thus avoiding anthropocentrism. As for circularity, it seems impossible to build a non-circular analysis of causation that is grounded on manipulation or intervention, insofar as both are forms of causation. Recent interventionist theories of causation such as Woodward's (2003) are explicitly intended not to be reductionist.[72]

Each of the directed edges in a causal net (as introduced earlier) represents the direct influence of a "parent" variable on a "child" variable. The dependence of a variable on its parent variables can also be represented, in a more precise way, by a structural equation. SEs provide an alternative and complementary tool for the construction of causal models, aside from probability distributions, which we saw earlier. Contrary to ordinary equations, SE are defined to be

---

[69] Spirtes et al. (2000), Pearl (2000), Woodward (2003), Sloman (2005), Fenton-Glynn (2021).

[70] Menzies and Price (1993, p. 187). Cf. Gasking (1955), Woodward (2009).

[71] Von Wright (1971) argues that although the fact that the human capacity to intervene in events in the experimental sciences is indispensable for the analysis of our *knowledge* of causal relations, we should not conclude from this that human action is essential to the *metaphysics* of causation.

[72] Woodward (2015a) takes the attempt of providing a reductive analysis of the concept of causation to belong to ontology$_2$/metaphysics$_2$, whereas ontology$_1$ suffices to account for the use of the concept of causation in science. Ontology$_1$ doesn't require the reduction of causation to other concepts.

asymmetrical: the SE of an "endogenous" variable V expresses the functional dependence of V on other variables in the model. A variable is called "exogenous" if its value is determined by factors external to the causal system whose model is being built.

SE have an interventionist interpretation and imply counterfactuals.[73] Let Y be a function of X, and let X and Y have the values $X=x_1$ and $Y=y_1$ in some actual situation. The SE $Y=f(X)$ entails that if X had some value $\neq x_1$, for example, x_2, Y would have the value $Y=y_2=f(x_2)$, and it entails that if an intervention set X to value x_2, Y would take value y_2.

Let me illustrate the construction of a causal net on the basis of structural equations with the biological case of preemption mentioned earlier, which presents a challenge to earlier counterfactual accounts.

A simple deterministic model can be built with the following binary variables:[74]

MA=1 microglia active; MA=0 microglia not active;
MR=1 microglia remove debris; MR=0 microglia don't remove debris;
AA=1 astrocytes active; AA=0 astrocytes not active;
AR=1 astrocytes remove debris; AR=0 astrocytes don't remove debris;
BW=1 brain without debris; BW=0 brain with debris.

Each endogenous variable is associated with a SE. To apply the model to a situation, one needs to specify the values of the exogenous variables. Set MA=1 and AA=1. The value of the endogenous variable MR is then determined by the value of MA, according to the SE $MR=f(MA)=MA$. If the microglia are active, they remove the debris (MA=1 and MR=1) and if they aren't, they don't (MA=0 and MR=0).

The preemption of the process beginning with active astrocytes is expressed by the SE for AR: $AR = \min (AA, 1-MR)$. The astrocytes remove the debris only if (1) the astrocytes are active and if (2) the microglia haven't removed the debris. The variable BW representing the state of the brain is also endogenous: $BW = \max (MR, AR)$. The brain is free of debris either because the microglia have removed the debris or because the astrocytes have removed them.

The content of the set of SE can be represented in a graph (Figure 3), where each variable corresponds to a node in the graph. An arrow from variable X to variable Y represents the fact that the value of Y depends on the value of X; in

---

[73] Hitchcock (2001, p. 280). It is possible to take account of both deterministic and probabilistic counterfactual dependence.

[74] A probabilistic model using variables with continuous values would be more realistic.

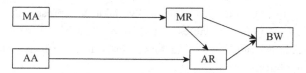

Figure 3 Graph representing a causal net.

this case, X is called a "parent" of Y. A *directed path* from X to Y is a sequence of adjacent arrows leading from X to Y.

Each arrow and each SE represents a set of counterfactual conditionals. Once a model is constructed, it can be used to determine the truth-value of new counterfactuals that do not simply correspond to one arrow. Say we want to know what would have happened if the microglia, though active, would some-how not have removed the debris. To find this out, one sets the variable corresponding to the antecedent of the counterfactual to the value it would have if the antecedent were true. In this case, one sets MR=0. This represents an "atomic intervention" (Pearl 2000, p. 70). One does not take into consideration the past that might have led to the truth of the antecedent. Rather, the value of the antecedent (here, MR) is set while the values of all variables corresponding to the past of the antecedent keep the values they actually have. In the graphical representation, this means that all arrows leading to the variable MR are erased, which is equivalent to transforming MR into an exogenous variable.

In the interventionist interpretation of this formalism, this corresponds to a localized experimental intervention on variable MR, which originates from outside the system and is direct in the sense that it is not obtained indirectly by intervening on factors that influence MR within the system.[75]

---

[75] Interventions perform a conceptual role similar to Lewis' "miracles" (1979/1986, p. 44). An intervention on a hypothetical cause variable C with respect to a hypothetical effect variable E is usually required to be "atomic" or "surgical" in the sense that the intervention does not at the same time modify any other variables. (This is possible if direct links between variables are "modular." See Hausman and Woodward (2004)). All variables in the model, which are possible "confounders," that is, independent causes of E, must be "controlled," that is, kept at their actual value. With the experimental techniques that are presently available, and for most variables, it is very difficult to intervene on them, in this technical sense. Practically possible interventions are often both "soft" and "fat handed" (Eberhardt and Scheines 2007; Baumgartner and Gebharter 2016; Eronen 2020). In a soft intervention, the intervention does not completely determine the cause variable, which remains influenced by its ordinary causes. In a fat-handed intervention, the experimental intervention modifies several variables at the same time. It is practically impossible to control for all other variables, as soon as the model gets sufficiently rich to hold promise of representing relevant causal connections. This problem can to some extent be overcome by the method of randomized controlled trials. However, in a model that contains both psychological variables and physiological variables that represent the ground of those psychological variables, interventions are necessarily fat-handed because psychological variables "supervene" (Kim 1993; McLaughlin and Bennett 2018) on their physiological grounds. See Section 9.3. It has been argued (Baumgartner 2010, 2013) that interventionist methods of research for causes are

Just as Lewis' miracles, this conception of interventions guarantees that no "backtracking" counterfactual can be true. When the value of variable X is modified, the variables situated upstream from X are left untouched. In the standard representation, these are the variables figuring at the left of X. The values that the variables downstream from (i.e., to the right of) X take in a situation in which X takes the stipulated value can then be determined on the basis of the equations corresponding to the arrows starting at X.

Pearl (2000, p. 70) defines the causal effect of X on Y, written "P(y/do(x))," as the probability distribution of the different values y of Y, given that an intervention ("do") has set variable X to the value x. This has the consequence that all factors different from X that also influence Y are included in X's impact on Y. To avoid this result, Woodward (2003, p. 98) imposes additional constraints on interventions I appropriate to determining whether X causes Y.[76] (1) I causes X. (2) I is the only cause of X, in the sense that all other influences on X are cut. (3) I does not cause Y through any paths that do not go through X. Say we want to find out whether the calculating activity of my computer (X) heats it up (Y). If I, the intervention of switching the computer on, not only triggers X but also turns on the cooler Z, I is not an intervention on X in the technical sense of Woodward's conditions, for whether the value of Y is changed by I does not only depend on X but also on Z. In particular, the fact that Y doesn't vary when I varies (because the heating influence of X on Y is offset by the cooling influence of Z on Y) does not justify the conclusion that X doesn't influence Y. (4) I is statistically independent of all variables Z that influence Y through paths that do not go through X. If, in order to find out whether the indication X of a barometer causes thunderstorms Y, my interventions I on X depend on (my knowledge of) air pressure Z, then Y may vary as a function of the values that I imposes on X, whereas X does of course not cause Y.

Causal models built from SE can be used to define *different concepts* of causal influence. The concept of an *actual cause* is illuminating in situations of preemption.[77] In the situation represented by Figure 3, BW depends

---

insufficient to discover causal relationships in models that contain both psychological and physiological variables, or variables that stand in other forms of non-causal dependence. Modifications to the interventionist criteria may make interventionism applicable to such models (Woodward 2015; Baumgartner and Gebharter 2016; Craver, Glennan, and Povich 2021). Soft and fat-handed interventions often suffice to experimentally justify or confirm causal claims (Woodward 2015a, p. 3594; Craver 2021, p. 156/7; Friend 2021, Friend forthcoming).

[76] These conditions make explicit the conditions of well designed experiments aimed at finding out whether X causes Y.

[77] The concept of actual cause is intended to express, within the framework of SE, the notion of singular cause, or token cause, as opposed to generic cause or type-level cause. In a situation where X is a cause of Y at the level of types of events, represented by variables X and Y, the question of whether a singular event belonging to type X causes a singular event belonging to

counterfactually neither on MA nor on AA. However, it would be wrong to conclude that neither MA nor AA causes BW. Indeed, in each situation, either one or the other causes BW. The concept of actual cause can be used to justify the intuition that MA is the cause of BW in situations where MA=1, although BW doesn't depend counterfactually on MA.

MA taking value 1 (MA=1) is *an actual cause* of BW=1. X=1 is an actual cause of Z=1 if and only if there is an "active causal route" (Hitchcock 2001, p. 287) from X to Z in an appropriate causal model $<V, E>$. A "route" between X and Z in the set V is an ordered sequence of variables $<X, Y_1, \ldots, Y_n, Z>$ such that each variable in the sequence is in V and is a parent of its successor in the sequence. The route $<X, Y_1, \ldots, Y_n, Z>$ is *active* in the causal model $<V, E>$ if and only if Z depends counterfactually on X within the new system of equations E' constructed from E, by setting the values of all variables that do not lie on the route to their actual values (Hitchcock 2001, p. 286).

In our example, MA=1 comes out as an actual cause of BW=1 because, if AR, which does not lie on the route from MA to BW is set to its actual value, that is, 0, BW counterfactually depends on MA.[78]

The structural equations framework provides the means for distinguishing different causal notions that can all be expressed by the common-sense word "cause." This shows the fecundity of this approach, although it cannot provide a non-circular analysis of causation. As we have seen earlier, a variable can influence another variable in two independent ways in such a way that these influences cancel each other out. Switching on (S) the calculating activity X of my computer raises its temperature Y,[79] but it also causes the onset of the cooling system Z, which lowers its temperature. It is possible that the positive direct influence of X on Y is exactly compensated by the negative influence of Z on Y, so that S has zero net influence on Y.[80] In such a case, it seems intuitively both correct to say that switching the computer on heats it up and that it doesn't heat it up. However, this involves no paradox insofar as the two judgments contain different notions of cause.[81] The former is correct if "heats it up" is taken to express the concept of being a *contributing* cause, the latter is correct if "heats it up" is taken to express

---

type Y, can be expressed by the question of whether the fact that X has value x (X=x) is an actual cause of the fact that Y has value y (Y=y). Cf. Hitchcock (2001), Woodward (2003), Halpern and Pearl (2005). I will use Hitchcock's terminology. See Section 6.1.

[78] The concept of actual causation and its definition with the help of the concept of an active route build on Lewis' concept of quasi-dependence (Lewis 1986, p. 206).

[79] Hesslow (1976) gives a structurally similar example.

[80] This possibility is precluded in the construction of Bayes nets by the Faithfulness condition. See Section 2.

[81] Cf. Woodward (2003, p. 50ff.).

the concept of being a *total* cause. In the situation sketched, S is not a "total cause" of Y but S is a "contributing cause" of Y.

(TC) X is a total cause of Y if and only if there is a possible intervention on X that will change Y or the probability distribution of Y (Woodward 2003, p. 51).

(CC) X is a contributing cause of Y with respect to a set of variables V, if and only if (1) there is a directed path from X to Y so that each variable on the path directly influences its immediate descendant, and (2) there is an intervention on X that changes the value of Y if the values of all variables in V that do not lie on that path are held fixed at some value (Woodward 2003, p. 57).

Indeed, if we hold Z in our example fixed, we find that an intervention on X modifies the value of Y, so that S is a contributing cause of Y, although the application of condition (TC) shows that it is not a total cause of Y: if Z is not held fixed, switching on the computer does not make its temperature rise.

Older versions of the manipulability theory make the judgment "X causes Y" depend on the possibility of acting on X. This seems to make it impossible to apply the concept of causation to events that are in principle outside the sphere of influence of human interventions. However, eruptions of volcanoes and explosions of supernovae are causes although no possible human action could ever bring them about or modify them. The notion of intervention solves this problem because it is defined without any reference to human action. Analyses of causation in terms of structural equations and directed graphs avoid anthropocentrism because the intervention that sets the value of the putative cause need not be the result of a human action. Natural events entirely independent of intentional actions can satisfy the formal conditions on an intervention modifying the value of the putative cause. Such "natural experiments"[82] provide just as good a basis for judging causal influence as intentional interventions by human experimenters. In neuropsychology, the hypothesis that the activation X of one brain region causally influences the activation Y of another brain region is confirmed by the observation that a modification of X due to accident or illness is systematically followed by a modification of Y.

However, there seem to be causal relations on which even interventions as defined in this sense seem to be impossible. To judge whether the gravitational attraction of the moon causally influences the tides, one must examine the consequences of an intervention on the position or the mass of the moon. It can be doubted whether interventions on the moon are physically possible: such

---

[82] Bernard (1865/2008, p. 112).

an intervention would require modifying the position or the mass of the moon by some means that does not also *directly* influence the tides.[83]

The clearest limit to the applicability of the concept of intervention concerns cosmology. The possibility of an intervention on a system requires the system under study to be smaller than the whole universe because the origin of an intervention on some system must lie outside that system.[84]

Interventions provide a strong epistemic criterion for causal influence. However, we have seen that it may not always be possible, even in principle, to carry out interventions in the required sense. Even if interventionist conditions are sufficient, they are not necessary for causation. In this respect, the interventionist account does not provide a complete metaphysical theory of causation.

6 Methodological Interlude

We have had a look at four reductive approaches to causation and at the framework of causal models, which can be interpreted with the conceptual tools of earlier accounts (lawful regularity, conditional probability, counterfactual dependence, intervention) so as to yield a powerful formal method for representing causal knowledge and the search for causes. Before I introduce and evaluate the approach to causation in terms of physical processes linking spatiotemporally localized particular events, let me make some methodological remarks.

6.1 Type and Token Causation

Approaches in terms of regularities, laws, counterfactuals, and manipulation were first introduced as theories of causation between particular events. However, accounts in terms of conditional probabilities represent relations of causal influence between factors or types of events. Causal models, on the basis of Bayes nets or structural equations, were also initially developed as representing causal influence between types of events. The variables that occupy the nodes of causal nets and that are related by SE have initially been interpreted as representing types of events. However, it is possible to build models of causal

---

[83] Woodward (2003, p. 129/30). It is impossible to find out by intervention whether the age at which children start school influences their scholarly performance. Given that performance is also influenced (independently of schooling) by chronological age, the appropriate intervention is impossible: it would consist in modifying the age at which children enter school while holding fixed their chronological age (Woodward 2015a, p. 3592/3). In many situations, it does not seem possible to construct useful models in which it is possible to satisfy the interventionist constraint that the intervention on X with respect to Y be "atomic" or "surgical," that is, not influence other variables Z (in addition to X) that lie on causal paths towards Y. This problem might be overcome by modifying the conditions imposed on interventions (Woodward 2015, p. 333; Friend 2021; forthcoming).

[84] "If you wish to include the entire universe in the model, causality disappears because interventions disappear" (Pearl 2000, p. 349/50). Woodward (2007, p. 69/70; 2009, p. 257).

influence among particular events, with the help of the concept of actual causation. In models of actual causation, values of variables, rather than those variables themselves, play the role of the terms of causal influence.

In causal models, causation relates variables or values of variables. It may seem straightforward to conclude that "it is most perspicuous to think of causal relationships as relating *variables*" (Woodward 2003, p. 39; italics in original). However, in the context of a metaphysical enquiry into causation as a feature of reality, it is crucial to note that variables are a representational device, which are created and postulated together with models by human model-builders. If a model correctly represents some part of reality, these variables represent features of reality. If a model contains variables X and Y with a direct edge pointing from X to Y, then if the model represents reality correctly, there are features of reality represented by X and Y so that the feature represented by X causally influences the feature represented by Y. Causation can be studied both at the level of types of events and at the level of particular events. Causal dependence at the level of token events does not reduce to causal dependence at the level of types of events, yet these dependence relations are not independent of each other either.

No consensus has been reached concerning the notion of event that is most appropriate for understanding causation among particular events (Gallow 2022). Events can be construed in coarse-grained and fine-grained ways. According to a coarse-grained construal, an event is the content of a space-time zone (Quine 1985), whereas according to a fine-grained construal (Kim 1976), events are triples, constituted by an object, a property and a time. Take Davidson's (1969/1980, p. 178) example of a metal ball that rotates and gets warmer simultaneously. According to the coarse-grained conception, the ball's warming up and the ball's rotating are two properties of the same event; whereas they are constitutive of two different events in the fine-grained conception. The structure of such fine-grained events is analogous to that of facts. One can distinguish between the fact that the ball warms up and the fact that it rotates; these facts (and the corresponding fine-grained events) have different causes and effects.

The distinction between type-level and token-level causation may shed light on the controversy over whether omissions and preventions can be causes. Is Alice's omitting to water Ben's plants a cause of their death?[85] It is much more natural to construe omissions as facts rather than as events. Causal propositions in which the cause and/or the effect is/are a negative fact(s) are incompatible with three intuitive properties of causation noted by Hall (2004): a causal

---

[85] The example is Beebee's (2004).

process is local (in the sense that the cause is linked to the effect by an intermediate series of events), intrinsic (it does not depend on what happens or is the case elsewhere), and transitive. If *a* can cause *b* by omission or prevention, then certain causal relations obey neither to locality nor to intrinsicality nor to transitivity. Three (incompatible) consequences can be drawn from this.

1 Omissions and preventions are not instances of causation although they appear to us as such, because we often conflate causal and non-causal dependence and explanation or because we conflate causation and moral responsibility.[86]

2 Omission and prevention are forms of causation, which means that locality, intrinsicality, and transitivity are not after all necessary conditions for causation (Schaffer 2000/2004).

3 There are two concepts of causation or two aspects of the concept of causation: One corresponds to dependence between variables (associated with nomological dependence, counterfactual dependence, and probability raising), the other corresponds to the existence of a transmission process at the level of particular events.[87] Omission and prevention are causal according to the first concept but not the second.

One way of resolving this debate is to interpret omission statements as expressing type-level dependence at the level of variables. Omissions and other negative facts can be represented by values of variables, just as "positive" facts. However, omission statements do not directly make reference to relations between particular events. Rather, they give counterfactual information about *possible* causal relations among events,[88] often with implicit information about norms or rules: Alice has promised to water Ben's plants, and if she hadn't omitted to water them, they wouldn't have died. There is a difference making relation between the omission and the plants' death, which violates the norms of promises.

The distinction between causation at the level of particular events and causal influence at the level of factors or types can also shed light on the question whether causation is intrinsic. A stone thrown against a window followed by the window's breaking it is one of philosophers' favorite examples of causation. The thesis that causation is intrinsic means that only facts determined locally at the spatiotemporal region stretching from the stone throw to the window

---

[86] Armstrong (1999), Dowe (2000, chap. 6, 2001), Beebee (2004), Mumford and Anjum (2010, p. 155). See Section 8.5.

[87] According to Hall (2004), these two concepts of causation are independent of each other.

[88] Hart and Honoré (1959/1985, p. 38) argue that omission statements describe the world by contrast. Dowe (2000; 2001) argues that omissions are not causation but "causation*."

breaking determine whether this is a case of causation, or merely a case of non-causal succession.

The thesis that causation is intrinsic is plausible for causal relations between particular events.[89] Whether or not c causes e is determined exclusively by spatiotemporally localized events c and e and the space-time region between them. However, accounts of causation in terms of difference-making at the level of types of events entail that causation is not intrinsic. This is clear for regularity theories: Whether or not the stone breaks the window is not determined only by what happens in the spatiotemporal surrounding of the stone's impact and the window's breaking, but by regularities concerning what happens to other events elsewhere in time and space.[90]

Another controversial question is whether causation has a contrastive struc-ture rather than the structure of a relation or a process between events (Schaffer 2005). A contrastive causal claim is that c rather than c* causes e rather than e*. This idea can be analyzed in an interventionist framework, in terms of two interventions, the first setting the value of a cause variable to c, the second setting it to c*. The contrastive claim then expresses the fact that the first intervention leads to the effect variable taking value e, whereas the second leads to its having value e*.

6.2 Conceptual Analysis and Metaphysics of Science

Theories of causation may pursue one of several aims.[91] They may aim at analyzing (a) the common-sense (or "folk") notion of causation (as in Lewis' theory of causation in terms of counterfactual dependence), (b) representations of causation in human minds, together with the nature and psychological mechanisms of causal reasoning,[92] (c) the concept of causation as it is implicit in scientific methods, and made explicit in algorithms for constructing Bayes Nets and causal models, (d) what causation is in reality.

Here is a straightforward way to see the difference between theories that aim at analyzing the concept of causation and theories of what causation is in reality. Theories of the former sort are intended to apply not only to reality but also to possibilities: Our concept of causation puts us in a position to understand causation as it occurs in fairy tales, in science fiction novels and films, and

---

[89] Menzies (1996, p. 98); Lewis (1986, p. 205), Hall (2004). Woodward (2014, p. 704, 2015a, p. 3598) suggests that the presence of a process connecting the cause to the effect makes causal relations typically more stable than causal relations without any process, such as omissions or double preventions, and that the fact that such stability is useful may explain the intuition that processes are necessary for causation.

[90] Carnap (1966/1995, p. 203).

[91] Paul (2009), Menzies (2009), Woodward (2014, 2015a), Kistler (2014).

[92] Gopnik and Schultz (2007), Waldmann (2017).

more generally causation as it could be. We easily understand fairy tales in which magicians transform princes in frogs, even if their spells act at a temporal and spatial distance without any intermediate processes. Theories of causation as it is in the real world have nothing to say on magical causation, but they must at least in part be informed by contemporary science, whereas theories of concepts of causation are not so restricted. The distinction has implications for their respective criteria of adequacy: theories about the *concept* of causation are assessed by a priori criteria. They must be coherent in light of other concepts and intuitions; they can be refuted by thought experiments or situations featuring conceptually possible events and processes, such as magical spells, teletransportation, or time travel. They *cannot* be refuted by their incompatibility with what physics tells us about physically possible influences. By contrast, theories of causation as it is in the real world are assessed by empirical criteria and can only be refuted by being incompatible with scientific facts or theories concerning the real world.

One can express the difference between the aims of such theories in terms of two interpretations of metaphysics. Theories like (a) and (b), which aim at analyzing the concept of causation, can be seen as belonging to descriptive metaphysics (Strawson 1959), which aims at describing the structure of reality as it is according to common sense. Theories of causation as it is in the real world (d) can be taken to belong to the metaphysics of science.[93] Causal models (c) can be interpreted in both ways. The application of the so-called "Canberra plan" (introduced in Section 8), which consists in trying to provide a functional reduction of the concept of causation, integrates both conceptual analysis and empirical hypotheses, and attempts to achieve the objectives of both descriptive metaphysics and metaphysics of science. Woodward (2021a) shows how and why the enquiry of what causation is "in the world" is inseparable from inquiries about how we humans think about causation, how we go about finding out about what causes what and how we use that knowledge for manipulating the world.[94]

7 Processes and Mechanisms

We have examined accounts of causation in terms of regularity, probability raising, counterfactual dependence, intervention, and causal models. The first

---

[93] Ney (2012), Schrenk (2016). Guay and Pradeu (2020) situate the distinction between descriptive metaphysics and metaphysics of science within a rich array of distinctions.

[94] All four aims I have distinguished can be pursued within the framework of what Woodward (2015a) calls "ontology$_1$," without making use, in the sense of Woodward's metaphysics$_2$/ontology$_2$, of any specifically metaphysical concepts, such as causal power or necessitation between universals, which are neither used in science nor part of common sense. Theories using such specifically metaphysical concepts are discussed in Section 3.

three of these suffer from counterexamples and the fourth cannot be applied in all situations. The approach in terms of causal models, which analyzes causation in terms of difference-making at the level of types of events, presupposes the distinction between causal and non-causal dependence.[95] Causal models are built under the constraint of using only variables that are "independently fixable," that is, that do not stand in non-causal dependence relations.[96] Therefore, they do not provide a framework that can be used to explain the difference between causal and non-causal dependence relations.

This distinction may be made at the level of particular events, on the basis of the empirical hypothesis that causation is a local physical process that stretches between two events that are localized in space and time. We will see that this empirical hypothesis can be used as a complement to accounts of causal influence in terms of causal models.

One historical source of process accounts of causation is Russell's (1948) analysis of causation in terms of "causal lines," which is inspired by the physical notion of a world line (Reichenbach 1928/1958). The world line of an object or process is its spatiotemporal trajectory. Russell defines a causal line as a world line that possesses qualities or structures that are either constant or change only smoothly (Russell 1948, p. 477). However, being a causal line is neither necessary nor sufficient for being a real causal process. It is not sufficient because the continuity of structure or quality can also characterize what Reichenbach calls an "unreal sequence" (Reichenbach 1928/1958, §23, p. 148) and Salmon (1984, p. 141ff) a "pseudo-processes." Pseudo-processes are world lines that give human observers the illusory impression of a causal process: they are not causal, but their qualitative continuity qualifies them as Russellian causal lines. Take Reichenbach's (1928/1958, §23, p. 148) fast rotating projector casting a spot of light on a distant wall so that the spot sweeps over the wall. The world line consisting of the series of places on the wall at the times at which the light spot appears on them is a causal line without being a causal process. It exhibits qualitative continuity but cannot be causal. This can be seen from the fact that its speed can exceed the speed of light if the distance between the projector and the wall is sufficiently large and the speed of rotation of the projector sufficiently fast. Each spot at x at t is the end point of a causal process originating in the projector, without having any influence on the

---

[95] For an attempt to account for the distinction between causal and non-causal dependence in a causal modeling framework, in terms of supervenience, see Hoffmann-Kolss (2022).

[96] "All pairs of variables in the model are independently fixable; i.e., it is metaphysically possible for both variables to be set to any combination of their individually possible values by independent interventions" (Woodward 2015, p. 316). Yang (2013), Weslake (forthcoming). It is controversial whether this requirement can or should always be satisfied (Williamson 2009, p. 200; Kistler 2013; Friend 2021).

adjacent spot. Being a causal line is not necessary for being a causal process either. Some causal processes lack continuity of structure and exhibit large and fast qualitative changes, for example, when several particles of different types follow each other in a "cascade" of radioactive decomposition (see Section 2).

Salmon (1984) has combined Russell's and Reichenbach's analyses, suggesting that a causal process is a process that (1) has structure or qualities that are either permanent or only changing continuously and (2) is capable of transmitting a mark, which is defined as a local modification of structure.[97] The light spot gliding along the wall is not a causal process because, if one modifies its color by inserting a red filter between the projector and the wall at one point, this modification will not propagate to the subsequent world line of the spot.

This analysis in terms of continuity of structure and mark transmission raises several difficulties.[98] The mark transmission criterion is shown to be insufficient by pseudo-processes capable of transmitting marks. Kitcher (1989, p. 463) mentions derivative marks: when a passenger in a car holds a flag out of the window, the shadow cast by the car as it passes along a wall bears the mark of the flag. Moreover, the analysis of the notions of mark and of causal interaction seems to be circular:[99] A mark is a modification of structure introduced into a process by a causal interaction, but an interaction is causal if it leads to the introduction of a mark.

An alternative proposal characterizes a causal process as a world line along which some physical quantity is transmitted or transferred, such as energy, momentum,[100] or more generally, some conserved quantity.[101] Processes construed in terms of transference can be used to justify causal judgments that challenge difference-making accounts. If active microglia preempt active astrocytes in cleaning the brain of debris, there is no (chain of) counterfactual dependence between active microglia and the cleaning of debris. Transference accounts suggest that what grounds the fact that the microglia's activity causes the cleaning of debris is that there is a physical process transmitting energy and momentum to the debris in the microglia's case, but not in the astrocytes'. However, the latter claim can be challenged. Given that there is physical transmission everywhere (except for events that are spacelike separate in the sense of relativity theory), the astrocytes also transmit physical quantities to the debris.

---

[97] Reichenbach has introduced the concept of a mark as a criterion for distinguishing between cause and effect (Reichenbach 1928/1958, §21, p. 136; 1956).

[98] These difficulties have led Salmon (1994/1998) to abandon it.   [99] Dowe (1992, p. 200/1).

[100] Aronson (1971), Fair (1979).

[101] Salmon (1994/1998), Kistler (1998, 1999/2006, 2021). The idea to characterize causation in terms of conserved quantities is due to Dowe (1992, 2000), but Dowe (1995, p. 370, 2000, p. 58) argues that amounts of conserved quantities cannot be transferred.

Or take the radioactive decay of nuclei of the isotope ^{223}Fr of Francium (see Section 2). This case refutes accounts of causation in terms of probability raising because the probability of having an effect of type ^{219}Rn is lower given the cause (there being a nucleus of type ^{219}At) than given the alternative possibility that it be of type ^{223}Ra. It seems doubtful whether interventions can be used to overcome this difficulty. But transference of energy and other conserved quantities provides a ground for the judgment that the decay of a ^{219}At nucleus causes the coming into being of a ^{219}Rn nucleus. More generally, transference justifies causal judgments in cases where (1) the cause belongs to a type that lowers the probability of events of the type of the effect, (2) cause and effect are categorized in terms of types that have only one member, so that probabilistic approaches are inapplicable.

The hypothesis that causation is grounded on a process of transmission fits the intuitions of locality and intrinsicality, according to which the existence of a causal relation between *a* and *b* only depends on processes stretching from *a* to *b*. Difference-making accounts, in terms of nomological dependence, probability raising, counterfactuals, or in terms of causal models, run counter that intuition. They all construe causation as non-intrinsic.

Challenges against the hypothesis that causation is grounded on transference can be grouped in two sorts. Objections of the first sort are based on considerations having to do with the content of physical theory; they accept the project of finding out what causation is in the real world according to science, but object to the hypothesis that it is transference of an amount of a conserved quantity. The second type of challenge is conceptual and based on counterexamples: cases of causation without transference or cases of transference without causation. Let me look at the former challenges first.[102]

1. In order to give sense to the idea that something x is transferred from a to b, x must persist over time. It can be questioned whether particular quantities of conserved quantities, such as energy, can persist through time like substances.[103] However, the statement that an amount q of energy (or some other conserved quantity) is transferred between space-time regions A and B, where events a and b are located, can be justified without requiring

---

[102] Another objection is that the Aharonov-Bohm effect is incompatible with the transference hypothesis. Ardourel and Guay (2018), Kistler (2021).

[103] Quine (1973, p. 6), Ehring (1986, p. 256), Dieks (1986). This objection has led Dowe (1992, 2000) to elaborate a version of the process theory of causation that avoids requiring transmission. In Dowe's account, a causal process is a world line characterized by the "continuous manifestation" of a conserved quantity in the physical sense, such as energy. His account is vulnerable to the objection Salmon has raised against Russell's account in terms of causal lines. Certain pseudo-processes, such as a spot of light gliding over a wall, manifest conserved quantities, without thereby being causal. See Salmon (1994/1998, p. 257); Kistler (1998); (1999/2006).

that q is a substance. A necessary and sufficient condition for the transference of energy (or another conserved quantity) between A and B is the existence of a time-like or light-like curve connecting these regions along which a field carrying energy (or another conserved quantity) is propagated.

2. In the framework of the theory of general relativity, it is not possible to derive a generally valid form of the conservation of energy. However, the notion of transmission presupposes that of conservation: only what is conserved can be transmitted. Therefore, transference of energy cannot be what makes true causal propositions bearing on large scale cosmological events, for example, that the big bang is the distant cause of the present expansion of the Milky Way, or on events in regions with non-negligible space-time curvature (Curiel 2000; Lam 2005). That leaves open the possibility that transference provides a necessary and sufficient *local* condition for causation between events that are situated in approximately flat regions of space-time.

3. A third argument against the transference hypothesis relies on the existence of non-local dependencies in entangled systems in quantum mechanics. In a variant of the experiment first conceived by Einstein, Podolsky and Rosen (1935), two electrons are prepared in an entangled singlet state of spin ½, and then move in opposite directions. According to quantum mechanics, measurements of a given component of the spins of such entangled pairs of particles are strictly correlated. Whether or not the results of the measurements are determined before the measurements (as hidden-variable theories assume) or not (as the orthodox version of quantum mechanics assumes), the result of one measurement seems to have an instantaneous causal influence at a distance on the other measurement. If causation is grounded on transference, the dependence of one measurement on the other in an EPR-style experiment cannot be causal. The non-causal character of the dependence of one result of measurement on the other can also be brought out by the fact that it is impossible to manipulate one result by intervening on the other.[104] The correlations between measurement events on entangled pairs of particles that are spacelike separated may be cases of non-local and non-causal determination.[105]

4. A necessary and sufficient condition for the transference of energy (or other conserved quantities) between A and B (according to the transference hypothesis, itself necessary and sufficient for causation) is the existence of

---

[104] Hausman and Woodward (1999, p. 565), Maudlin (2011), Woodward (2015a, p. 3588).

[105] Dowe (1996, p. 228/9) suggests that the measurements might be causally related after all, through backwards causation. Ardourel and Guay (2018, p. 14) suggest that the EPR correlation between the two measurements is no case of causation because that would require that the measurements are *two* events or bear on *two* systems. If the particles are entangled at the time of measurement, they are one system, not two.

a time-like or light-like curve connecting these regions along which a field carrying energy (or another conserved quantity) is propagated. This seems to make the account circular because "carry" and "propagate" are causal notions. Attempts to analyze the meaning of these causal notions in terms of transmission would either lead to an infinite regress or a vicious circle. It seems more promising to analyze the meaning of these expressions in terms of laws of nature. This yields a theory in two parts: (1) Causation is grounded on transference. (2) Transference of amounts of conserved quantities is grounded on laws of physics. The transference theory is a variant of the nomological theory because, at bottom, laws of physics ground causation. However, not any law of any type, or even any type of law of evolution, is sufficient for causation, as it is according to (DN-C). The only laws that ground causation are the laws of propagation of energy and other conserved quantities along time-like or light-light curves.

The fundamental role of laws raises two problems. (1) It threatens to make the account lose its locality and intrinsicality, which seemed to give it an advantage over non-local theories, such as causal models.[106] (2) If the relevant laws are reversible, the asymmetry of causation is not a consequence of the physical transmission process that grounds causation in the actual world, but has an independent ground,[107] such as the fact that our region of the universe contains many irreversible processes that are all oriented in the same direction, according to the second law of thermodynamics.[108]

Now let us look at challenges that have been raised against process accounts from a conceptual point of view.

5. Process theories take causation to be a type of relation or process whose characteristics can only be discovered by empirical research; they contain empirical hypotheses about what it is, physically, that makes a relation or process causal. Such hypotheses are fallible, that is, may turn out to be false on empirical grounds. That is a strength: after all, the fallibility of a theory proves that it is not tautological (Popper 1934). But the fact that these theories have empirical content can also been seen as a weakness: Contrary to theories that aim at analyzing causation in an a priori manner by pure conceptual analysis, an empirical theory aims only at correctly characterizing causation as it is in the real world.[109] One reply to this

[106] Hüttemann (2013, p. 132).   [107] Dowe (1992a, 1996), Ney (2009).

[108] Such a physical ground of the asymmetry of causation can also ground the direction of time. Reichenbach (1956), Lewis (1979/1986), Hausman (1998).

[109] "Assuming, as seems reasonable, that it is a contingent matter what the fundamental laws are, physical connection accounts cannot (because they are not designed to) tell us anything about

worry is that it is inappropriate to criticize process theories for not satisfying criteria that are not appropriate for them. An empirical theory of causation in reality has no ambition to account for all *possible* sorts of causation, in particular to those featuring in science fiction novels or fairy tales. Another reply is that process theory, although fallible as an empirical hypothesis, might well be, if it is true, necessarily true, in analogy with Kripke's thesis that the statement that water is H_2O is a posteriori, but nevertheless, if true, necessarily true.[110]

6. Another objection is that transmission processes are everywhere. Events that are spatiotemporally sufficiently close to each other are, for example, often linked by transmissions of photons. Therefore, transmission theory seems condemned to lead to a plethora of true causal judgments.[111] It can be replied first that those plethoric causal judgments are true but lack communicational relevance.[112] Second, the relevant causal processes can be chosen on perfectly objective grounds, on the basis of the properties of the effect that is indicated in the *explanandum* of the causal explanation one is looking for. If one asks for the cause of Peter's standing up, the relevant causal process is at the physiological and psychological level and leads to the instantiation of the physiological and psychological properties constitutive of standing up.

7. An objection to this latter reply is that the transference hypothesis applies only to physical causal processes and is thus inadequate to ground the truth of ordinary causal judgments involving non-physical, for example, psychological, properties. Mary asks Peter to stand up, and he stands up. The cause of Peter's standing up has to do with his understanding of the content of Mary's request but apparently it does not seem to be relevant to consider the underlying causal process from the point of view of energy transmission.[113] The transference hypothesis entails indeed that all causes and effects are physical. What the objection shows is that a satisfactory account of causation must take the influence of properties into account, over and above the

---

causation as it might have been – in particular, as it is in worlds with laws very different from our own. That limitation seems not merely unfortunate but deeply misguided" (Collins, Hall, and Paul 2004, p. 14).

[110] It is controversial whether "cause" is a natural kind term in the same sense as "water" (Bontly 2006; Kistler 2014, p. 81; Woodward 2021a, p. 142/3).

[111] Salmon (1994/1998, p. 258); Noordhof (2020, p. 316).   [112] Ney (2009).

[113] See Collins, Hall, and Paul (2004, p. 14). Here is Psillos' comment on Glennan's example of a "social mechanism whereby information is disseminated through a phone-calling chain" (Glennan 2002, S346). "It is surely otiose and uninformative to try to describe this mechanism in terms of exchange of conserved quantities" (Psillos 2004, p. 310). However, all parties agree that "the interactions involved in telephone calls supervene on basic physical interactions" (Psillos 2004, p. 310). What would be problematic is to seek or give a privilege to a causal *explanation* at a physical level, because higher-level phenomena are better explained by interactions and mechanisms at higher levels than physics. See Sections 9.3 and 9.4.

mere existence of causal relations based on transference. We will look at proposals for integrating the process account with causal models, in which the relevant properties are represented by variables, next.

8. Process accounts seem to be refuted by omissions and preventions. If I kill a plant by omitting to water it, it seems that I have caused its death without having transmitted anything to it.[114] If on the contrary I *prevent* the plant's death by watering it, the event of the plant's death does not take place and cannot therefore be the target of any transmission. Schaffer (2000/2004) argues that there are many common-sense causal propositions bearing on situations in which no transmission seems to be involved. Striking cases are propositions expressing double prevention (Hall 2004, p. 241), in which the cause prevents the prevention of an effect. In the operon theory of gene expression,[115] gene expression is triggered by an "inductor" molecule that prevents a "repressor" molecule from preventing it. Omission and prevention are forms of difference-making. In the next section, we will look at attempts to integrate processes with difference making.

8 Integrating Causal Models with Processes

We have seen that accounts in terms of (1) nomological deducibility, (2) conditional probabilities, (3) counterfactual dependence, (4) interventions, all yield fallible criteria for causation.[116] The framework of causal models can be interpreted using the conceptual tools of (1) – (4) so as to solve many of the problems of earlier accounts. However, causal models provide only a part of a complete theory of causation. The construction of a model presupposes the distinction between causal and non-causal dependence. A set of variables is appropriate for the construction of a causal model only if it doesn't contain any variables related by forms non-causal dependence. Otherwise, the variables do not respect "independent fixability."[117] Causal models do not provide a framework within which one could represent the question which dependence relations are causal, and which are logical, conceptual or metaphysical, because their construction presupposes an answer to that question.

---

[114] More precisely, I do not transmit anything relevant to the plant, although there are no doubt innumerable irrelevant processes linking me to it, such as transmission of photons.

[115] Schaffner (1993, chap. 3), Morange (2001).

[116] Hitchcock describes one sort of "methodological pluralism" about causation, according to which "the different philosophical theories of causation offer models of causation. Causation, on this view, would be something different from probability raising, counterfactual dependence, energy-momentum-transfer, or what have you; yet each [. . .] would [. . .] offer some helpful insights into the nature of causation [. . .] While each of the models of causation has its limitations [. . .] each model may be useful" (Hitchcock 2007, p. 205/6).

[117] See note 96.

Accounts in terms of mechanisms can be seen as complementary to difference-making accounts, and in particular to causal models. This complementarity can be seen from two sides. Pearl says that "each parent-child relationship in the network represents a stable and autonomous physical mechanism" (Pearl 2000, p. 22). These physical mechanisms are not characterized within causal models; rather, they can be interpreted as constituting the metaphysical reality that explains the functional dependence between variables expressed in structural equations and causal models. See Section 5.

Mechanisms have been introduced in the philosophy of causal explanation and causation as a reaction to the inadequacy of the DN model for the analysis of the scientific analysis of causation in the life sciences.[118] Accounts in terms of probability raising, counterfactuals, interventions, or causal models all seem inappropriate for causation in biology and neuroscience, where causal explanation does not in general rely on the discovery of exceptionless regularities, or manipulability at the level of variables, but on the discovery of mechanisms. There are at least two ways of analyzing the concept of a mechanism. One is Salmon's and Dowe's in terms of processes (see Section 7). A second analysis takes mechanisms to be systems of interacting parts.[119] "A mechanism underlying a behavior is a complex system which produces that behavior by the interaction of a number of parts according to direct causal laws" (Glennan 1996, p. 52). The direct links between variables in causal models can be interpreted in terms of mechanisms, which motivates the mechanistic theory of token level causation: "two events are causally related when and only when they are connected by an intervening mechanism" (Glennan 2009, 316).[120]

So here is one aspect of the complementarity of causal models and mechanistic accounts: Causal models and other difference-making theories represent networks of causal links between variables, and mechanistic theories aim at identifying the metaphysical processes that underlie each direct link between variables (Glennan 2017, p. 168).

Here is a second way in which mechanisms and difference-making relations (corresponding to direct links between variables in causal models) complement

---

[118] Machamer, Darden, and Craver (2000).

[119] These two approaches to analyzing mechanisms use different concepts and are independent of each other. Philosophers who use the notion of a mechanism in their analysis of causation do not in general use the notion of process, as it is analyzed by Salmon and Dowe (Glennan 2017, chap. 7 shows how the two notions of mechanism can be articulated), and those who analyze causation in terms of processes, focusing often on causation in physics, do not in general use the notion of a mechanism in the sense in which is it used in the philosophy of the life sciences.

[120] See also Glennan (2002, 2017). The analysis is plausible in the life sciences and may be generalized to other sciences, but not to fundamental physics.

each other. Influence relations between variables representing higher-level features of, for example, biological systems, are "mechanically explicable" (Glennan 1996, pp. 61–3). They are the result of interactions between parts of the system. The interactions between parts that help explain a given causal link at level *n* lie at lower levels. The concept of levels of properties is controversial and can receive different interpretations. In a mereological interpretation, the properties of a whole object lie at a higher level than the properties of its parts.[121] In general, interactions at level *n-1* are themselves mechanically explicable in terms of still lower levels, *n-2* and beyond. One example is the multilevel mechanism of long-term memory (Craver 2007, pp. 165–70). The mechanistic account of causation is not reductive and must be completed by some complementary account of what makes true the most fundamental interactions. The account of the fundamental account may be in terms of laws of nature, as Glennan (1996) and Psillos (2004) suggest, or in terms of direct causal influence between variables in causal models (Woodward 2011). Fundamental influence relations may be grounded on transference.

The complementarity of difference-making and mechanistic/process accounts must not be confused with pluralism, according to which "cause" is a polysemic word that is ambiguous between different concepts. For pluralism, what is meant by a causal statement depends on the context. Many varieties of pluralism are conceivable and many forms have been explored.[122] It is undeniable that there exist several causal concepts, all useful in certain contexts and irreducible to one another, such as direct and indirect cause, or contributing and total cause. The complementarity thesis just sketched is very different from the pluralist claim that causal statements like "smoking causes cancer" are ambiguous and express either the concept of causation as difference-making or the concept of causation as process or mechanism.[123]

The application to causation of the so-called "Canberra plan"[124] provides another important way to conceive of the complementarity of difference-making

---

[121] In a *reductionist* sense of "level," if some laws of science S_1 can be reduced in terms of science S_2, the properties and laws of S_1 lie at a higher level than those of S_2. Craver calls mereological levels "levels of composition" (Craver 2007, p. 184) and reductionist levels, "levels of science" (Craver 2007, p. 172). Eronen (2015) argues that the concept of level is misleading because it is ambiguous between an interpretation referring to composition and an interpretation referring to size scale.

[122] Hitchcock (2007), Psillos (2004, 2009), Hall (2004).

[123] It also differs from epistemic forms of pluralism according to which we know causation by various aspects, characteristics, or symptoms (Reiss 2009; Williamson 2009). According to Williamson's "epistemic theory," both mechanisms and probabilistic dependencies are "indicators of causality" (Williamson 2009, p. 209). Both types of evidence are arguably needed in science, and in particular in medicine and epidemiology, to fully justify statements like "smoking causes cancer."

[124] Jackson (1998), Papineau (2020).

accounts (such as causal models) and process accounts (Lewis 1994a, 2004; Menzies 1996; Bontly 2006). The Canberra plan is a general strategy for the naturalization of philosophical concepts, that is, for integrating common-sense notions with scientific knowledge. It is in part conceptual and in part empirical. In a first a priori step, the content of a concept is derived from ordinary common-sense intuitions or "platitudes" about the correct application of the concept: The concept is characterized in terms of a "functional role." In a second, empirical step, scientific knowledge is used to produce a hypothesis about what in reality plays the functional role identified in the first step. Kim offers the example of the biological notion of a gene. In the first step the functional role corresponding to the notion of gene is identified as "that mechanism in a biological organism causally responsible for the transmission of heritable characteristics from parents to offsprings" (Kim 1998, p. 25). In the second step, (parts of) DNA molecules are identified as what fills the role.

Applying this strategy to causation, a first step identifies the conceptual role corresponding to the notion of cause. It is plausible that this conceptual role can be characterized by virtue of all or some subset of "the central connotations of causation" (Schaffer 2000a, p. 289) I have mentioned at the very beginning of this Element.[125] The second step consists in making a hypothesis, informed by science, about what fills the role identified in the first step. Menzies mentions as one promising hypothesis for the filler of the role described by the folk concept of causation, Fair's (1979) proposal that "the causal relation is the relation of transfer of energy-momentum from cause to effect" (Menzies 1996, p. 104).

One worry is that the Canberra plan takes the functional role identified in the first step to be a causal role.[126] This makes it seem impossible to apply the reduction procedure to the concept of causation itself. But the role identified by a concept need not be a *causal* role. More substantial worries are that there are no clear-cut and universally shared intuitions about causation,[127] and that these intuitions are not purely a priori because they are in part shaped by what science tells us about possible role-fillers at the second step.

Another proposal is that causation at the level of particular events is analyzed in a first step in physical terms, in terms of mechanisms or processes of

---

[125] Menzies calls the set of the first three features "the postulate of folk psychology" (Menzies 1996, p. 97). See Norton (2003, p. 15).

[126] Price (2001, p. 114).

[127] Hitchcock (2003), Illari and Russo (2014, p. 204/5); Bontly suggests that the application of the Canberra plan to causation might use "not [. . .] a list of a priori platitudes, but [. . .] our best psychological theory of causal judgement" (Bontly 2006, p. 195).

transference, and that we select, in a second step, from the vast number of physical causal relations, those that make a difference, in terms of probability raising, counterfactuals or causal models. According to "causal foundationalism" (Ney 2009), difference-making causation between events at the level of types results from our selecting those among the physical causal relations that are important for our purposes of explanation, prediction and action.

According to the complementarity thesis, there are two components in what makes true ordinary causal statements such as "Bob's coughing caused Carol's waking" (Glennan 2010, p. 365). (1) A physical process between the relevant particular events and (2) a difference-making relation at the level of relevant types under which these events fall, that is, in this case coughing and waking.[128] Both aspects of causation are required: on one hand "the spatiotemporal aspects of causation" (Hitchcock 2007, p. 214), on the other hand, the fact "that effects depend upon their causes, or that causes make a difference for their effects" (Hitchcock 2007, p. 214). What makes it true that c's being F is causally responsible[129] for e's being G, has two parts: there is a physical process linking c and e; 2) F makes a difference to G. The types by which events make a difference are in general not physical, but in a physicalist framework, it is supposed that all facts supervene[130] on the set of physical facts. If this is correct, the process of Bob's coughing waking Carol up supervenes on a physical process.[131]

9 Contemporary Debates

9.1 Grounding and Causation

One common thread that runs through modern philosophy of science is the idea that modern science replaces causation with functional dependence. We have seen earlier that causation can be construed as a particular form of dependence. But there are many non-causal forms of dependence.[132]

---

[128] Accounts of causation in terms of two complementary aspects have been proposed by Kistler (1999/2006), Glennan (2002), Psillos (2004), Ney (2009).

[129] Kistler (1999/2006, p. 163).

[130] Roughly, a first set of properties (or predicates) M is said to "supervene" on a second set P if and only if it is impossible that two objects differ with respect to a property of set M, without differing with respect to any property of set P. Physicalism is the doctrine according to which the set of mental properties supervenes on the set of physical properties. Several concepts of supervenience have been elaborated. One important difference between them concerns the interpretation of the concept of necessity (or impossibility) that is used in their definition. Cf. Kim (1990), McLaughlin and Bennett (2018).

[131] Dowe mentions this as a problem because it "requires commitment to a thoroughgoing reductionism" (2009, p. 224). However, it only requires supervenience, which is, contrary to reductionism, not controversial.

[132] Kim (1974), Huneman (2010), Lange (2016), Reutlinger and Saatsi (2018),

Grounding is a very general concept of dependence that has recently been the focus of much research in logic and metaphysics.[133] Grounding is formally defined as a relation of strict partial ordering, that is, one that is asymmetric, irreflexive, and transitive.[134] It applies to both formal (or logical) and empirical forms of dependence. The propositions p and q (logically) ground together the conjunction p∧q. Two H atoms and one O atom, when in a bound state, together (empirically) ground an H_2O molecule. Both the grounding of a conjunction on its terms and the grounding of a molecule on its component atoms are non-causal, even though the latter is a form of empirical, not conceptual, dependence. Grounding can be represented by structural equations, just as causation, because grounding and causation are both forms of dependence.[135] However, this is not enough to show that causation is a sort of grounding[136] or that grounding is a form of causation: "metaphysical causation."[137] The latter thesis modifies the traditional concept of causation, so that it can encompass many forms of dependence usually opposed to causation. It thereby abolishes the useful distinction between causal and non-causal dependence.[138]

9.2 Eliminativism with Respect to Causation in Physics

It has often been claimed that the concept of cause is obscure and anthropomorphic and has no place in science. "There is no cause nor effect in nature; nature has but an individual existence; nature simply *is*" (Mach 1960, p. 483; italics in original). "The reason why physics has ceased to look for causes is that, in fact, there are no such things" (Russell 1912/1919, p. 180). According to Mach and Russell, the use of the concept of cause results from anthropomorphic prejudice.

> [M]any imagine they understand motions better when they picture to themselves the pulling forces; and yet the *accelerations*, the facts, accomplish more, without superfluous additions. I hope that the science of the future will discard the idea of cause and effect, as being formally obscure; and in my feeling that these ideas contain a strong tincture of fetishism, I am certainly not alone. (Mach 1894, p. 254; italics in original)

"The word 'cause' is so inextricably bound up with misleading associations as to make its complete extrusion from the philosophical vocabulary desirable" (Russell 1912/1919, p. 180).

Eliminativists argue that the concept of cause should not be used in a worldview informed by science because in contemporary science,

---

[133] McKenzie (2022).
[134] Rodriguez-Pereyra (2015) and Thompson (2018) argue that grounding is not asymmetric, so that there can be mutual grounding.
[135] Schaffer (2016).   [136] Bennett (2017) calls it "building."   [137] Wilson (2018).
[138] Wilson (2014), Koslicki (2016).

"the concept of cause is replaced [. . .] by the concept of function" Mach (1960, p. 555).[139] Russell's claim that the most developed parts of physics do not use causal vocabulary is incorrect,[140] but it remains controversial whether the use of causal vocabulary should be interpreted literally. The fact that formulas and mathematical models don't have any causal characteristics does not show that physical theories have no causal content: Causation might be part of the interpretation of the formulas and models, which is required to use them to predict and explain real phenomena.[141]

Here are two arguments for why the functions expressed by equations used in physics cannot be interpreted causally:[142] (1) Causation is local, but according to classical mechanics it is the state of the whole universe that determines what happens at a given instant. (2) Causation is asymmetrical but no such asymmetry can be found in the laws. Classical mechanics and at least parts of quantum mechanics are time reversible. The state of the universe at a given time determines its state at other times, both in the past and in the future.

In reply, instead of concluding that physics gives us grounds to think there is no causation in physical nature, we may conclude that physics give us reasons to revise our intuitive concept of causation. Causation is less local than we might have expected. Here are two proposals for articulating the symmetry of fundamental physics with macroscopic asymmetrical causation. (1) David Albert (2000) proposes that macroscopic asymmetry of causation can be explained by the "past-hypothesis" (which says that the entropy of the universe was much lower in the very distant past than it is now) and statistical mechanical principles, although fundamental laws are time-symmetric. (2) Price and Ismael[143] argue that the asymmetry of macroscopic causation is "perspectival." Instead of being a metaphysical feature of the world, it results from a projection of the asymmetry of deliberation onto the world, which appears only to agents like ourselves.

It is generally accepted that causation is indispensable in practice and plays a major role in all applications of science, such as engineering. Causal knowledge is indispensable for finding effective strategies (Cartwright 1979). However, it is controversial whether certain physical theories contain or imply causal hypotheses, in particular linear response theory, and special and general relativity.[144]

---

[139] Russell (1903, p. 478; 1912/1919, p. 190, 194/5).

[140] Suppes (1970), Hitchcock (2007a), Ross and Spurrett (2007).   [141] Frisch (2012, 2014).

[142] Russell (1912/1919), Field (2003), Lange (2009), Blanchard (2016).

[143] Price (2007), Price and Weslake (2009), Ismael (2016).

[144] Frisch (2009; 2014) claims that this is the case in linear response theory, but Norton (2009) denies it. According to Reichenbach (1956) and Torretti (1983), physicists' talk about the "causal structure of spacetime in special relativity" (Wald 1984, p. 188) can be interpreted realistically. See Hoefer (2009). Against this, Norton argues that what might appear as

Causal eliminativism with respect to physics seems incompatible with causal realism with respect to models that are developed outside fundamental physics, given the (partial) unity of science (Tahko 2021), and in particular the existence of reduction relations (Nagel 1961). If causal models are interpreted realistically, how could causation "emerge" as a relation of variables outside of fundamental physics, although the variables of the special sciences supervene on those of physics? The tension can be resolved in an instrumentalist and pragmatic way by interpreting causal models as tools for prediction, not to be taken as descriptions of reality (Hitchcock 2007a, p. 52).[145] Moreover, it has been suggested that the tools provided by causal models have no application in fundamental physics.[146]

Eliminativist and antirealist arguments often rely on controversial assumptions. Such arguments can be criticized by showing that those assumptions can be dropped.

1) Norton (2003, p. 3) suggests that if causation were real it would have to be analogous to energy. However, causation can be realistically interpreted without postulating the existence of "causity"[147] as a type of substance or quantity, analogous to energy.

2) Many authors argue that a realistic interpretation of causation is incompatible with quantum mechanics because causation requires necessitation of the effect by the cause.[148] This assumption is dropped by probabilistic accounts.

3) Russell does not clearly distinguish between the claim that there are causes and the truth of the "law of causality" or "principle of causality," "the principle 'same cause, same effect'" (Russell 1912/1919, p. 188).[149] Causal realism is compatible with abandoning the law of causality.

4) Norton (2003, p. 8) suggests that the fact that classical mechanics is not a deterministic theory entails that there are "uncaused events" and "acausality" in classical physics. Probabilistic accounts, such as causal models, show that the concept of causation is independent of determinism. Counterfactual and process accounts are compatible with the existence of events to which classical mechanics doesn't even attribute any probability.[150]

---

constraints that relativity theory imposes on physically possible processes "are best understood as devices for cataloging the different ways that the light-cone structure may be spread globally over space-time" (Norton 2007, p. 228). Cf. Kistler (2021).

[145] According to Norton's causal "anti-fundamentalism" (Norton 2003), causal models should not be interpreted realistically because causation belongs to "folk science."

[146] "Fundamental physics is not a hospitable context for causation" (Woodward 2009, p. 257). See also Woodward (2014, p. 702); Glennan (1996, p. 68).

[147] The term is Castañeda's (1984).

[148] "The law of causality is no longer applied in quantum theory" (Heisenberg 1958, p. 88).

[149] Hitchcock (2007).　　[150] Wysocki (2023).

9.3 The Challenge against Mental and "Downward" Causation from Closure and Exclusion

The idea that the mind causally influences the physical world is often claimed to be incompatible with physicalism.[151] Physicalism is the doctrine according to which (1) everything is either physical or exclusively composed of physical parts, and (2) all properties of all objects supervene on the physical properties of those objects.[152] According to the construal of physicalism in terms of supervenience, mental properties, events, and processes are distinct from physical properties, events, and processes.

Kim (1998, 2005) argues that downward causation is incompatible with this construal of physicalism: It can never be literally correct that a mental event causes a physical event, because the causes of physical events are always exclusively physical.[153] If the argument were sound, it might be generalized to argue for the inefficacy of all higher-level causes.[154]

1) (Closure) *The causal closure of the physical domain.*[155] If a system p has at t_1 a physical property R, then there is, at each time t_0 preceding t_1, a physical property N such that the fact that p has N at t_0 is causally responsible[156] for the fact that p has R at t_1.

2) (Exclusion) *Principle of causal exclusion.*[157] If the fact that p has N at t_0 is causally responsible for the fact that p has R at t_1, there cannot be any property M distinct from N, and in particular no property M at some level higher than N, such that p has M at t_0 and such that the fact that p has M at t_0 is also causally responsible for the fact that p has R at t_1.

---

[151] See Maslen, Horgan, and Daly (2009), Robb, Heil, and Gibb (2023).

[152] There are stronger versions of physicalism, such as reductionism and eliminativism. According to the former, all real properties are reducible to physical properties, and according to the latter, strictly speaking, there are only physical properties. According to these strong forms of physicalism, the question whether the mind influences the physical world does not really arise, either because there is no mind (eliminativism) or because the mind is physical itself (reductionism).

[153] Here I use the term "event" in Kim's sense, as the instantiation of a property by some object at some time. See Sections 6.1 and 9.4. I shall consider the same question (whether mental properties can influence physical properties) in terms of structural equations.

[154] Kim (1997), Block (2003), Kim (2005). The concept of level has been introduced in Section 8.

[155] For critical discussion of closure, see Lowe (2000), Hendry (2017, p. 160), Orilia and Paolini Paoletti (2017).

[156] Causal responsibility has been introduced in Section 8.

[157] (Exclusion) is weaker than Kim's "principle of explanatory exclusion," which he later calls the "principle of determinative/generative exclusion" (Kim 2005, p. 17), according to which "two or more complete and independent explanations of the same event or phenomenon cannot coexist" (Kim 1989, p. 250). Kim's principle is not plausible because one fact can have both a causal and a non-causal explanation, both complete, which can be independent of each other (Kistler 2016, p. 250).

3) *No downward causation.* Therefore, no higher-level level property M is such that the fact that p has M at t_0 is causally responsible for the fact that p has R at t_1.

This result is troubling because it seems obvious that its conclusion is wrong and that our minds do influence physical events. My thoughts (M) cause my fingers to move over the keyboard (R) at this moment. It also seems to be incompatible with the scientific exploration of downward influence from psychological on physiological features of persons, for example, in the study of physiological effects of psychotherapy.[158]

Both Closure and Exclusion can be challenged. Closure, which is also called the principle of the "completeness of the physical," is regularly challenged in the context of the defense of emergentism.[159] Against Exclusion, it may be argued that mental (and other higher-level properties) can exercise their own autonomous causal influence, in parallel with the influence of their physical supervenience base.[160] It may also be argued that higher-level variables (or properties) can be efficacious by being identical with underlying physical variables (Heil and Robb 2003), or because they are composed of causal powers that are a subset of the causal powers of the underlying physical properties (Shoemaker 2007; Wilson 2011).

9.4 Robust and Proportional Causation

In the preceding section, we have considered an important challenge to the conceivability of mental causation. Mental events seem to be unable of influencing both physical and mental events, because any such influence is always exclusively due to the physical events underlying those mental events. One strategy for answering that challenge and thus justifying the possibility that mental events are causes merits a closer look,[161] if only because it also has other fruitful applications, for example, in biology (Woodward 2010). Dependence relations can be conceived in different ways. If Y depends on X, and if the dependence relation can be mathematically represented as functional dependence between variables, one can further distinguish whether the dependence is robust (or stable), and whether it is proportional (or specific). Both of these features are connected to the usefulness of knowing them for providing causal explanations and making causal predictions.

Take a causal model M that contains variables X and Y, so that X directly causally influences Y. Direct causation can be defined with the help of the notion

---

[158] Barsaglini et al. (2014).   [159] Wilson (2021).
[160] Mills (1996), Bennett (2003), Yang (2013), Weslake (forthcoming). See Section 9.4.
[161] Yablo (1992), Woodward (2008), Kistler (2017, 2021a).

of a counterfactual intervention (Woodward 2010). X causes Y if and only if, for some set of values of all other variables in set M, that is, in set $B = M\backslash\{X, Y\}$, if an intervention set the value of X to a different value from its actual value, the value of Y, or the probability distribution of Y, would change.

The *stability* or *robustness* of the causal influence of X on Y can be defined with respect to the range of the values of the variables in B, for which the influence of X on Y exists.[162] Stability comes in degrees: the causal influence of X on Y is the more stable the larger the set of values of B variables for which it persists. If X causes Y indirectly through a chain of intermediate variables X_1, X_2, ..., where each direct link between adjacent variables is less than perfectly stable, the indirect (or distal) causal influence of X on Y will in general be less stable than each direct link, and will in general be the less stable the longer the chain. This may be one source of the intuition that causation is not always transitive. But causation must not be confused with stable causation. A defender of transitivity, such as Lewis, can argue that long chains preserve causal influence, though they have little stability. The relative instability of causal relations between variables in biology may be used to justify the thesis that there are no laws in biology, or the weaker thesis according to which such laws are "system laws" (Schurz 2002), which hold only under special circumstances, characterizing what Cartwright calls "nomological machines" (Cartwright 1999), whereas "laws of nature" or fundamental laws are more stable.[163]

Another important concept is proportional causation. Let me introduce this concept with Yablo's (1992, p. 257) example of a pigeon that has been conditioned to peck at all and only red targets. It reliably pecks at all targets of all shades of red but not at any targets of any other color. Now consider a type of situation in which a scarlet target is shown and in which the perception of that scarlet target causes the pigeon to peck. If P is a variable whose values represent pecking and not pecking, the influence of the pigeon's perception of a colored target on P can correctly be represented both (1) in a model in which R is a variable whose values represent the perception of a red target and the absence of such a perception, and (2) in a model in which S is a variable whose values represent the perception of a scarlet target and the absence of such a perception. In the former model (1) is true, in the latter model, (2) is true:

(1) R causes P (*perception of red* target causes the pigeon to peck).
(2) S causes P (*perception of scarlet* target causes the pigeon to peck);

---

[162] David Lewis calls robust causal relationships "insensitive" (1986, p. 184).
[163] Lange (2009), Kistler (2006/2020).

However, (1) seems intuitively "more correct" than (2) because (1) "furnishes a better explanation" than (2) (Woodward 2010, p. 298). The difference between (1) and (2) can be explained in terms of proportionality. R is proportional to P, whereas S is not. Each modification of the value of R leads to a modification of the value of P,[164] whereas this is not the case for S with respect to P. Some modifications of the value of S do not lead to any change in the value of P: if the value of S is switched from scarlet to some non-scarlet shade of red, this will not change the value of P.

Mental and other higher-level causes may be proportional to their effect, whereas the underlying physical causes are not.[165] Thus, mental and other higher-level variables can be (1) causes, in parallel to underlying lower-level variables, and (2) more relevant for causal explanation than those underlying lower-level variables.[166]

9.5 Degrees of Causation

Most events have more than one cause. Often, it seems possible to compare different factors influencing the same event according to the strength of their influence. This can be important for many reasons, scientific, medical, moral, or legal. The issue can be raised both with respect to particular events and with respect to types of events. Take a river that is polluted by the sewage of several chemical plants. A scientific question bears on the contribution of each pollutant on different aspects of the modification of the ecosystem and in particular on the populations, or death, of animals and plants of various species. A medical issue is the contribution of each source of pollution to the incidence of certain diseases in the population living downstream who drink or otherwise use the polluted water. Moral and legal issues arise when it comes to determine the

---

[164] The proportionality of X with respect to Y can be defined with the help of the concept of injectivity. A function is *injective* iff for all pairs of values $x_i \neq x_j$, $f(x_i) \neq f(x_j)$, or in other words, there is no pair of values $x_i \neq x_j$ with $f(x_i) = f(x_j)$. In model (1) above, the function P=f(R) is injective, whereas the function P=f(S) is not. David Lewis' (2000/2004) concept of "influence," similar to Woodward's "fine-grained influence conception of specificity" (2010, p. 302), is defined by a weaker requirement: X counts as influencing Y, even if the function Y=f(X) is not injective, as long as it is not the case that $f(x_i) = f(x_j)$ for all values $x_i \neq x_j$ of the cause variable X (Lewis 2000/2004, p. 94/5). A stronger notion is Woodward's "specificity in the one to one sense" (2010, p. 313): the causal influence of X on Y is one-to-one specific if the function Y=f(X) is surjective, that is, both injective and surjective. A function Y=f(X) is surjective iff, for every value y_i of Y, there is a value x_j of X such that $y_i = f(x_j)$.

[165] It would be a mistake to judge, as List and Menzies (2009), but not Woodward (2010, p. 288) do, that all causation is proportional. See Kistler (2017), McDonnell (2017), Woodward (2015a, p. 3595/6; 2021).

[166] The proportionality requirement has been challenged for various reasons. See Bontly (2005), Hoffmann-Kolss (2014), Franklin-Hall (2016), Vaassen (2022).

amount of moral and legal responsibility of each of the polluting plants for the damage to people's health and to the ecosystem.

Several conceptual frameworks make room for the introduction of a concept of degree of causation or strength of causal influence.[167] Several measures of degrees of causal influence have been offered within the framework of probabilistic theories of causation.[168]

However, Sartorio argues that "the appearance that causal contributions come in degrees is just an illusion" (Sartorio 2020, p. 346), on the basis of her analysis of a "puzzle about the relationship between degrees of causation and degrees of responsibility" (Bernstein 2017, p. 165). Degrees of causal influence and degrees of moral responsibility are closely connected. Other things being equal, the amount of moral responsibility of an agent for an outcome seems to be "proportionate" (Bernstein 2017) to the degree to which the agent's actions caused that outcome.[169] The puzzle arises from the fact there seem to be two incompatible criteria for evaluating moral responsibility. To take Bernstein's example, in a first situation ("Victim"), two assassins independently kill a victim by shooting at her exactly at the same time, where the bullet shot by each is alone sufficient for her death. A second situation ("Hardy Victim") resembles the first in all respects but for the fact that both bullets are necessary for the victim's death, none of the individual bullets shot by the two assassins being alone sufficient (either because the bullets are weaker or because the victim is stronger).

According to one criterion for degrees of causal influence of an agent for an outcome, an action is more of a cause of a given outcome to the extent that it comes closer to being a *sufficient* condition for that outcome. According to another criterion, an action is more of a cause of a given outcome to the extent that it comes closer to being a *necessary* condition for that outcome.[170]

---

[167] Lewis' "causation as influence" comes in degrees (Lewis 2000/2004, p. 92). One might consider measuring degrees of causal influence in process accounts of causation by the quantity of energy or other conserved quantity that is transferred. However, it seems more plausible to use transference as a criterion for whether there is a causal link at all, and introduce the concept of degree of influence as a modification of the difference making component of the concept of causation. See Kaiserman (2018, p. 10, note 15).

[168] Suppes (1970), Eells (1991), Lewis (1986). See Fitelson and Hitchcock (2011). These measures are not in general equivalent to each other, although some are (Sprenger 2018).

[169] Causal judgments are influenced by what people consider to be typical or normal. Subjects are more likely to judge that someone's action causes an outcome if that action violates some policy or other norm (Knobe and Fraser 2008; Hitchcock and Knobe 2009). Given that normality admits for degrees, these judgments will attribute degrees of causation (Halpern and Hitchcock 2015).

[170] Kaiserman (2018) suggests that the criterion in terms of sufficiency seems appropriate according to the "production intuition" (Kaiserman 2018, p. 9), whereas the second seems appropriate according to the "dependence intuition" (Kaiserman 2018, p. 10), in the sense of Hall's (2004) distinction.

The puzzle arises from the fact that the two criteria sometimes yield incompatible verdicts: according to the sufficiency criterion the assassins are more of a cause of the death in Victim than in Hardy Victim because each is sufficient in Victim but not in Hardy Victim, whereas the opposite holds according to the necessity criterion: each assassin is more of a cause in Hardy Victim because her contribution is necessary for the death, which is not the case in Victim.

There are at least two strategies to react to the puzzle, which both preserve the existence of degrees of causation. One strategy is to hold that the puzzle arises only in the field of judgments of moral responsibility, whereas closeness to sufficiency is the only appropriate measure of degree of causation.[171] Another strategy is to accept that the puzzle concerns intuitive judgments of causal influence but that this is just one more case in which there are several causal concepts, each of which comes with its own degrees of causal influence.[172]

10 Concluding Remarks

This Element began with the observation that causation is crucial for our conception of the world and ourselves, from the perspective of both common sense and science, but that its philosophical analysis remains controversial. So far, all efforts to elaborate a reductive account able to account for all uses of the concept of causation have failed. This has led many authors to abandon the attempt at finding a unique reductive analysis. Various forms of pluralism have been explored according to which there are many concepts of causation. One form of pluralism consists in interpreting various concepts of causation as so many conceptual tools that are useful in limited contexts. The strategy of elaborating causal concepts as tools has proven very fruitful in the framework of formal methods of causal modeling. These formal methods have allowed making much progress in elaborating different concepts of causation, such as contributing and total cause, direct and indirect cause, and actual cause. It has become clear that the failure to elaborate a reductive account is no obstacle to our improving our understanding of causation. In particular, it has turned out that one gets a better grasp on the concept of cause by clearly understanding various types of situations that have been obstacles to all simple reductive accounts, such as cases involving omissions, preventions, and cases where causation doesn't seem to be transitive. Just as important is progress that brings into sharp focus unresolved issues that constitute challenges for future philosophical research on causation. Here are two of them.

Most contemporary philosophers accept both that causation, understood with the help of formal models such as structural equations and causal nets, is crucial

---

[171] Hoffmann-Kolss and Rolffs (2024).   [172] This strategy is suggested by Demirtas (2022).

for science and common sense and that causation has no place in physics. But how can there be causation in our ordinary life, and in chemistry, biology, psychology, economy and the law, if there is no physical causation? It seems difficult to reconcile this in particular with the widely accepted, and often presupposed, physicalist worldview, according to which all events and processes described in terms of the concepts of common sense or in the terms of some science other than physics, depend on physical events and processes. The tension is certainly alleviated once reductionism is abandoned: if one abandons the thesis of logical empiricism that all other sciences are in principle reducible to physics, there is no contradiction in holding both that there is no causation in physics and that there is causation everywhere else although everything depends in some sense on physics. But there remains a tension. This tension is apparent in arguments for eliminativism in the philosophy of mind, with respect to cognitive states and events. According to the so-called exclusion argument, cognitive states and events cannot be causes because their causal powers are excluded by the causal powers of the physiological and physical states of the cognitive systems entertaining these cognitive states. This argument presupposes that those underlying physical states have causal powers. Therefore, it is incompatible with the thesis that there is no physical causation.

Another topic that awaits further exploration is the distinction between causal and non-causal dependence. The construction of causal models presupposes this distinction because causal nets can only be built with variables that are chosen so that, for each pair of variables, there are only two possibilities: either they are independent of each other or they stand in a relation of causal influence. Variables must be chosen so that they do not depend on each other in any other way: a causal model must not contain variables that stand in logical, conceptual or supervenience relations, or that are related by non-causal association laws. Thus, the possibility of analyzing causation in terms of causal models depends on the distinction between causal and non-causal dependence. However, no generally accepted account of this distinction has yet emerged. From a metaphysical point of view, what is needed is a theory of what makes properties or events independent enough of each other so as to be able to stand in causal relations. Only variables that represent properties or events of that sort are appropriate for use in structural equations and causal nets. The challenge is to find a non-circular way of distinguishing causal and non-causal dependence and of characterizing various non-causal forms of dependence. As long as the choice of variables that are appropriate for causal models remains outside of philosophical accounts of the elaboration and use of such models, our understanding of causation remains incomplete.

References

Albert, David Z. (2000), *Time and Chance*, Cambridge, MA: Harvard University Press.

Andersen, Holly (2013), When to Expect Violations of Causal Faithfulness and Why It Matters, *Philosophy of Science* 80, pp. 672–683.

Anjum, Rani Lill and Mumford Stephen (2018), *Causation in Science and the Methods of Scientific Discovery*, Oxford: Oxford University Press.

Anjum, Rani Lill and Mumford Stephen (2018a), *What Tends to Be: The Philosophy of Dispositional Modality*, London: Routledge.

Appleton, David R., French, Joyce M., and Vanderpump, Mark P.J. (1996), Ignoring a Covariate: An Example of Simpson's Paradox, *American Statistician* 50, pp. 340–341.

Aronson, Jerrold J. (1971), On the Grammar of "Cause", *Synthese* 22, pp. 414–430.

Ardourel, Vincent and Alexandre Guay (2018), Why Is the Transference Theory of Causation Insufficient? The Challenge of the Aharonov-Bohm Effect, *Studies in History and Philosophy of Modern Physics* 63, pp. 12–23.

Armstrong, David M. (1978), *Universals and Scientific Realism, Volume 2: A Theory of Universals*, Cambridge: Cambridge University Press.

Armstrong, David M. (1983), *What Is a Law of Nature*, Cambridge: Cambridge University Press.

Armstrong, David M. (1997), *A World of States of Affairs*, Cambridge: Cambridge University Press.

Armstrong, David M. (1999), The Open Door: Counterfactual Versus Singularist Theories of Causation, in Sankey, Howard (ed.), *Causation and Laws of Nature*, Dordrecht: Kluwer, pp. 175–185.

Armstrong, David M. (2004), *Truth and Truthmakers*, Cambridge: Cambridge University Press.

Barsaglini, Alessio et al. (2014), The Effects of Psychotherapy on Brain Function: A Systematic and Critical Review, *Progress in Neurobiology* 114, pp. 1–14.

Baumgartner, Michael (2010), Interventionism and Epiphenomenalism, *Canadian Journal of Philosophy* 40, pp. 359–384.

Baumgartner, Michael (2013), Rendering Interventionism and Non-Reductive Physicalism Compatible, *Dialectica* 67, pp. 1–27.

Baumgartner, Michael and Alexander Gebharter (2016), Constitutive Relevance, Mutual Manipulability, and Fat-Handedness, *British Journal for the Philosophy of Science* 67, pp. 731–756.

Beebee, Helen (2004), Causation and Nothingness, in Collins, John, Ned Hall, and L. A. Paul (eds.), *Causation and Counterfactuals*, Cambridge, MA: MIT Press, pp. 291–308.

Beebee, Helen, Christopher Hitchcock, and Peter Menzies (eds.) (2009), *The Oxford Handbook of Causation*, Oxford: Oxford University Press.

Bennett, Jonathan (1988), *Events and Their Names*, Oxford: Oxford University Press.

Bennett, Karen (2003), Why the Exclusion Problem Seems Intractable, and How, Just Maybe, to Tract It, *Nous* 37, pp. 471–497.

Bennett, Karen (2017), *Making Things Up*, Oxford: Oxford University Press.

Bernard, Claude (1865/2008), *Introduction à l'étude de la médecine expérimentale*, Paris: Librairie Générale Française, 2008. English transl.: *An Introduction to the Study of Experimental Medicine*, New York: Henry Schuman, 1927.

Bernstein, Sara J. (2017), Causal Proportions and Moral Responsibility, in David Shoemaker (ed.), *Oxford Studies in Agency and Responsibility, Volume 4*, Oxford: Oxford University Press, pp. 165–182.

Bird, Alexander (2010), Causation and the Manifestation of Powers, in Anna Marmodoro (ed.), *The Metaphysics of Powers: Their grounding and their manifestation*, New York: Routledge, pp. 160–168.

Blanchard, Thomas (2016), Physics and Causation, *Philosophy Compass* 11, pp. 256–266.

Block, Ned (2003), Do Causal Powers Drain Away? *Philosophy and Phenomenological Research* 67, pp. 133–150.

Bontly, Thomas (2005), Proportionality, Causation, and Exclusion, *Philosophia* 32, pp. 331–348.

Bontly, Thomas (2006), What Is an Empirical Analysis of Causation, *Synthese* 151, pp. 177–200.

Borghini, Andrea, and Williams, Neil E. (2008), A Dispositional Theory of Possibility, *Dialectica* 62, pp. 21–41.

Bridgman, PercyWilliams (1927), *The Logic of Modern Physics*, New York: Macmillan.

Carnap, Rudolf (1931), Die Überwindung der Metaphysik durch logische Analyse der Sprache, *Erkenntnis* 2, pp. 219–241. Translated by A. Pap, The Elimination of Metaphysics Through Logical Analysis of Language, in A. J. Ayer, ed., *Logical Positivism*, Glencoe, Il: The Free Press, 1959, pp. 60–81.

Carnap, Rudolf (1966/1995), *An Introduction to the Philosophy of Science*, ed. M. Gardner (originally published as *Philosophical Foundations of Physics*, New York: Basic Books, 1966), New York: Dover, 1995.

Cartwright, Nancy (1979), Causal Laws and Effective Strategies, *Noûs* 13, pp. 419–437; Repr. in N. Cartwright (ed.), *How the Laws of Physics Lie*, Oxford: Clarendon Press, 1983.

Cartwright, Nancy (1989), *Nature's Capacities and Their Measurement*, Oxford: Clarendon Press.

Cartwright, Nancy (1999), *The Dappled World: A Study of the Boundaries of Science*, Oxford: Clarendon Press.

Cartwright, Nancy (2007), Hunting Causes and Using Them, Cambridge: Cambridge University Press.

Cassirer, Ernst (1910/1923), *Substanzbegriff und Funktionsbegriff* (1910), Translated by W. P. Swabey and M. C. Swabey, Substance and Function, in *Substance and Function and Einstein's Theory of Relativity*, LaSalle, Il: Open Court, 1923.

Castañeda Hector-Neri (1984), Causes, Causity, and Energy, *Midwest Studies in Philosophy* 9, pp. 17–28.

Chakravartty, Anjan (2013), Review of Mumford and Anjum, Getting Causes from Power, *British Journal for the Philosophy of Science* 64, pp. 895–899.

Collins, John, Ned Hall, and L. A. Paul (eds.) (2004), *Causation and Counterfactuals*, Cambridge, MA: MIT Press.

Craver, Carl (2007), *Explaining the Brain: Mechanisms and the Mosaic Unit of Neuroscience*, Oxford: Oxford University Press.

Craver, Carl (2021), Toward an Epistemology of Intervention: Optogenetics and Maker's Knowledge, in J. Bickle, C. Craver, A. S. Barwich (eds.), *The Tools of Neuroscience Experiments*, New York: Routledge, pp. 152–175.

Craver, Carl, Stuart Glennan and Mark Povich (2021), Constitutive Relevance and Mutual Manipulability Revisited, *Synthese* 199, pp. 8807–8828.

Curiel, Erik (2000), The Constraints General Relativity Places on Physicalist Accounts of Causality, *Theoria* 15, pp. 33–58.

Davidson, Donald (1967/1980), Causal Relations, in Davidson, *Essays on Actions and Events*, Oxford: Clarendon Press, pp. 149–162.

Davidson, Donald (1969/1980), The Individuation of Events, in Davidson, *Essays on Actions and Events*, Oxford: Clarendon Press, pp. 163–180.

Davidson, Donald (1970/1980), Mental Events, in Davidson, *Essays on Actions and Events*, Oxford: Clarendon Press, pp. 207–225.

Davidson, Donald (1995), Laws and Cause, *Dialectica* 49, pp. 263–279.

Demirtas, Huzeyfe (2022), Causation Comes in Degrees, *Synthese* 200, pp. 1–17.

Dieks, Dennis (1986), Physics and the Direction of Causation, *Erkenntnis* 25, pp. 85–110.

Dowe, Phil (1992), Wesley Salmon's Process Theory of Causality and the Conserved Quantity Theory, *Philosophy of Science* 59, pp. 195–216.

Dowe Phil (1992a), Process Causality and Asymmetry, *Erkenntnis* 37, pp. 179–196.

Dowe, Phil (1993), On the Reduction of Process Causality to Statistical Relations, *British Journal for the Philosophy of Science* 44, pp. 325–327.

Dowe, Phil (1995), What's Right and What's Wrong With Transference Theories, *Erkenntnis* 42, pp. 363–374.

Dowe, Phil (1996), Backwards Causation and the Direction of Causal Processes, *Mind* 105, pp. 1–22.

Dowe, Phil (2000), *Physical Causation*, Cambridge: Cambridge University Press.

Dowe, Phil (2001), A Counterfactual Theory of Prevention and "Causation" by Omission, *Australasian Journal of Philosophy* 79, pp. 216–226.

Dowe, Phil (2009), Causal Process Theories, in Helen Beebee, Christopher Hitchcock and Peter Menzies (eds.), *The Oxford Handbook of Causation*, Oxford: Oxford University Press, pp. 213–233.

Dretske, Fred (1977), Laws of Nature, *Phil. of Science* 44, pp. 248–268.

Ducasse C. J. (1926), On the Nature and Observability of the Causal Relation, in: Ernest Sosa and Michael Tooley (eds.), *Causation*, New York: Oxford University Press, 1993.

Ducasse, C. J. (1966), Critique of Hume's Conception of Causality, *Journal of Philosophy* 63, pp. 141–148.

Eberhardt, Frederick, and Richard Scheines (2007), Interventions and Causal Inference, *Philosophy of Science* 74, pp. 981–995.

Eells, Ellery (1991), *Probabilistic Causality*, Cambridge: Cambridge University Press.

Ehring, Douglas (1986), The Transference Theory of Causation, *Synthese* 67, pp. 249–258.

Einstein, Albert, Podolsky Boris and Rosen Nathan. (1935), Can Quantum-Mechanical Description of Reality Be Considered Complete? *Physical Review* 47, pp. 777–780.

Elga, Adam (2001), Statistical Mechanics and the Asymmetry of Counterfactual Dependence, *Philosophy of Science* (suppl.) 68, pp. S313–S324.

Ellis, Brian (2001), *Scientific Essentialism*, Cambridge: Cambridge University Press.

Eronen, Markus I. (2015), Levels of Organization: A Deflationary Account, *Biology and Philosophy* 30, pp. 39–58.

Eronen, Markus I. (2020), Causal Discovery and the Problem of Psychological Interventions, *New Ideas in Psychology* 59, 100785.

Fair, David (1979), Causation and the Flow of Energy, *Erkenntnis* 14, pp. 219–250.

Faye, Jan (2024), Backwards Causation, in: Edward N. Zalta and Uri Nodelman (eds.), *The Stanford Encyclopedia of Philosophy (Spring 2024 Edition)*, https://plato.stanford.edu/archives/spr2024/entries/causation-backwards/.

Fenton-Glynn, Luke (2012), Review of Mumford and Anjum, Getting Causes from Powers, *Mind* 121, pp. 1099–1106.

Fenton-Glynn, Luke (2021), *Causation*, Cambridge: Cambridge University Press.

Field, Hartry (2003), Causation in a Physical World, in Michael J. Loux and Dean W. Zimmerman (eds.), *The Oxford Handbook of Metaphysics*, Oxford: Oxford University Press, pp. 435–460.

Fitelson, Branden, and Christopher Hitchcock (2011), Probabilistic Measures of Causal Strength, in Phyllis Illari, Federica Russo, and Jon Williamson (eds.), *Causality in the Sciences*, New York: Oxford University Press, pp. 600–627.

Fodor, Jerry (1989), Making Mind Matter More, *Philosophical Topics* 17(1), pp. 49–71.

Franklin-Hall, Laura. R. (2016), High-Level Explanation and the Interventionists' Variables Problem, *British Journal for the Philosophy of Science* 67, pp. 553–577.

Friend, Toby (2019), Can Parts Cause Their Wholes? *Synthese* 196, pp. 5061–5082.

Friend, Toby (2021), Intervening on Time Derivatives, *Studies in History and Philosophy of Science* 89, pp. 74–83.

Friend, Toby (forthcoming), Soft Control: Furthering the Case for Modified Interventionist Theory, *Studies in History and Philosophy of Science*.

Frisch, Mathias (2009), "The Most Sacred Tenet"? Causal Reasoning in Physics, *British Journal for the Philosophy of Science* 60, pp. 459–474.

Frisch, Mathias (2012), Kausalität in der Physik, in Michael Esfeld (ed.), *Philosophie der Physik*, Frankfurt: Suhrkamp, pp. 411–426.

Frisch, Mathias (2014). *Causal Reasoning in Physics*, Cambridge: Cambridge University Press.

Gallow, J. Dimitri (2022), The Metaphysics of Causation, in Edward N. Zalta and Uri Nodelman (eds.), *The Stanford Encyclopedia of Philosophy* (Fall 2022 Edition), https://plato.stanford.edu/archives/fall2022/entries/causation-metaphysics/.

Garrett, Don (2009), Hume, in Helen Beebee, Christopher Hitchcock, and Peter Menzies (eds.), *The Oxford Handbook of Causation*, Oxford: Oxford University Press, pp. 73–91.

Gasking, Douglas (1955), Causation and Recipes, *Mind* 64, pp. 479–487.

Gebharter, Alexander (2017), *Causal Nets, Interventionism, and Mechanisms: Philosophical Foundations and Applications*, Cham: Springer.

Gebharter, Alexander and Retzlaff, Nina (2020), A New Proposal How to Handle Counterexamples to Markov Causation à la Cartwright, or: Fixing the Chemical Factory, *Synthese* 197, pp. 1467–1486.

Gillies, Donald (2000), Varieties of Propensity, *British Journal for Philosophy of Science* 51, pp. 807–835.

Glennan, Stuart (1996), Mechanisms and the Nature of Causation, *Erkenntnis* 44, pp. 49–71.

Glennan, Stuart (2002), Rethinking Mechanical Explanation, *Philosophy of Science* 69, pp. S342–S353.

Glennan, Stuart (2009), Mechanisms, in Helen Beebee, Christopher Hitchcock, Peter Menzies (eds.), *The Oxford Handbook of Causation*, Oxford: Oxford University Press, pp. 315–325.

Glennan, Stuart (2010), Mechanisms, Causes, and the Layered Model of the World, *Philosophy and Phenomenological Research* 81, pp. 362–381.

Glennan, Stuart (2017), *The New Mechanical Philosophy*, Oxford: Oxford University Press.

Gopnik, Alison and Laura Schulz (eds.) (2007), *Causal Learning: Psychology, Philosophy, and Computation*, New York: Oxford University Press.

Guay, Alexandre, and Thomas Pradeu (2020), Right Out of the Box: How to Situate Metaphysics of Science in Relation to Other Metaphysical Approaches, *Synthese* 197, pp. 1847–1866.

Haavelmo, Trygve (1943), The Statistical Interpretation of a System of Simultaneous Equations, *Econometrica* 11, pp. 1–12.

Hall, Ned (2004), Two Concepts of Causation, in Collins, John, Ned Hall, and L. A. Paul (eds.), *Causation and Counterfactuals*, Cambridge, MA: MIT Press, pp. 225–276.

Halpern, Joseph and Hitchcock, Christopher (2015), Graded Causation and Defaults, *British Journal for the Philosophy of Science* 66, pp. 413–457.

Halpern, Joseph Y., and Judea Pearl (2005), Causes and Explanations: A Structural-Model Approach, *British Journal for the Philosophy of Science* 56, pp. 843–887.

Hart, H. L. A. and Tony Honoré (1959/1985), *Causation in the Law, 2nd Ed.* Oxford: Clarendon Press.

Hausman, Daniel M. (1998), *Causal Asymmetries*, Cambridge: Cambridge University Press.

Hausman, Daniel M., and James Woodward (1999), Independence, Invariance and the Causal Markov Condition, *British Journal for the Philosophy of Science* 50, pp. 521–583.

Hausman, Daniel M., and James Woodward (2004), Modularity and the Causal Markov Condition: A Restatement, *British Journal for the Philosophy of Science* 55, pp. 147–161.

Healey, Richard (2009), Causation in Quantum Mechanics, in Helen Beebee, Christopher Hitchcock, and Peter Menzies (eds.), *The Oxford Handbook of Causation*, Oxford: Oxford University Press, pp. 673–686.

Heil, John and David Robb (2003), Mental Properties, *American Philosophical Quarterly* 40, pp. 175–196.

Heisenberg, Werner (1958), *Physics and Philosophy: The Revolution in Modern Science*, New York: Harper and Brothers.

Hempel, Carl G. (1965), *Aspects of Scientific Explanation: And Other Essays in the Philosophy of Science*, New York: The Free Press.

Hempel, Carl G. (1966), *Philosophy of Natural Science*, Englewood Cliffs, NJ: Prentice Hall.

Hendry, Robin (2017), Prospects for Strong Emergence in Chemistry, in Michele Paolini Paoletti and Francesco Orilia (eds.), *Philosophical and Scientific Perspectives on Downward Causation*, New York: Routledge, pp. 146–163.

Hesslow, Germund (1976), Two Notes on the Probabilistic Approach to Causality, *Philosophy of Science* 43, pp. 290–292.

Hitchcock, Christopher (1996), The Role of Contrast in Causal and Explanatory Claims, *Synthese* 107, pp. 395–419.

Hitchcock, Christopher (2001), The Intransitivity of Causation Revealed in Equations and Graphs, *Journal of Philosophy* 98, pp. 273–299.

Hitchcock, Christopher (2003), Of Humean Bondage, *British Journal for the Philosophy of Science* 54, pp. 1–25.

Hitchcock, Christopher (2004), Do All and Only Causes Raise the Probabilities of Effects?, in Collins, John, Ned Hall, and L. A. Paul (eds.), *Causation and Counterfactuals*, Cambridge, MA: MIT Press, pp. 403–417.

Hitchcock, Christopher (2007), How To Be a Causal Pluralist, in Peter Machamer and Gereon Wolters (eds.), *Thinking About Causes*, Pittsburgh: University of Pittsburgh Press, pp. 200–221.

Hitchcock, Christopher (2007a), What Russell Got Right, in Price and Corry (eds.), pp. 45–65.

Hitchcock, Christopher (2009), Causal Modeling, in Helen Beebee, Christopher Hitchcock, and Peter Menzies (eds.), *The Oxford Handbook of Causation*, Oxford: Oxford University Press, pp. 299–314.

Hitchcock, Christopher (2021) Probabilistic Causation, in Edward N. Zalta (ed.), *The Stanford Encyclopedia of Philosophy* (Spring 2021 Edition), https://plato.stanford.edu/archives/spr2021/entries/causation-probabilistic/.

Hitchcock, Christopher and Knobe, Joshua (2009), Cause and Norm, *Journal of Philosophy* 106, pp. 587–612.

Hoefer, Carl (2009), Causation in Space-Time Theories, in Helen Beebee, Christopher Hitchcock, and Peter Menzies (eds.), *The Oxford Handbook of Causation*, Oxford: Oxford University Press, pp. 687–706.

Hoffmann-Kolss, Vera (2014), Interventionism and Higher-Level Causation, *International Studies in the Philosophy of Science* 28, pp. 49–64.

Hoffmann-Kolss, Vera (2022), Interventionism and Non-Causal Dependence Relations: New Work for a Theory of Supervenience, *Australasian Journal of Philosophy* 100, pp. 679–694.

Hoffmann-Kolss, Vera, and Matthias Rolffs (2024), Graded Causation and Moral Responsibility, *Erkenntnis*.

Hume, David (1777/1975), An Enquiry Concerning Human Understanding, in ed. L. A. Selby-Bigge and P. H. Nidditch, *Enquiries Concerning Human Understanding and Concerning the Principles of Morals*, Oxford: Clarendon Press, 1975, Reprint 2003.

Huneman, Philippe (2010), Topological Explanations and Robustness in Biological Sciences, *Synthese* 177, pp. 213–245.

Hüttemann, Andreas (2013), *Ursachen*. Berlin: De Gruyter.

Illari, Phyllis, and Federica Russo (2014), *Causality. Philosophical Theory Meets Scientific Practice*, Oxford: Oxford University Press.

Ismael, Jennan (2016), How Do Causes Depend on Us: The Many Faces of Perspectivalism. *Synthese* 193, pp. 245–267.

Jaag, Siegfried, and Markus Schrenk (2020), *Naturgesetze*, Berlin: De Gruyter.

Jackson, Frank (1998), *From Metaphysics to Ethics: A Defence of Conceptual Analysis*. Oxford: Clarendon Press.

Kahneman, Daniel and Amos Tversky (1982), The Simulation Heuristic, in Kahneman, Daniel, Paul Slovic, and Amos Tversky (eds.), *Judgment under Uncertainty: Heuristics and Biases*, New York: Cambridge University Press, pp. 430–444.

Kaiserman, Alex (2018), 'More of a Cause': Recent Work on Degrees of Causation and Responsibility. *Philosophy Compass* 13, e12498.

Kant, Immanuel (1781/1998), *Critique of Pure Reason*, translated by Paul Guyer and Allen W. Wood, Cambridge: Cambridge University Press.

Kim, Jaegwon (1974), Noncausal Connections, repr. in *Supervenience and Mind*, New York: Cambridge University Press, 1993, pp. 22–32.

Kim, Jaegwon (1976), Events as Property Exemplifications, in M. Brand and D. Walton (eds.), *Action Theory*, Dordrecht: D. Reidel, pp. 159–177.

Kim, Jaegwon (1989), Mechanism, Purpose, and Explanatory Exclusion, repr. in *Supervenience and Mind*, New York: Cambridge University Press, 1993, pp. 237–264.

Kim, Jaegwon (1990), Supervenience as a Philosophical Concept, repr. in *Supervenience and Mind*, New York: Cambridge University Press, 1993, pp. 131–160.

Kim, Jaegwon (1993), *Supervenience and Mind: Selected Philosophical Essays*, Cambridge: Cambridge University Press.

Kim, Jaegwon (1997), Does the Problem of Mental Causation Generalize? *Proceedings of the Aristotelian Society* 97, pp. 281–297.

Kim, Jaegwon (1998), *Mind in a Physical World: An Essay on the Mind-Body Problem and Mental Causation*. Cambridge, MA: MIT Press.

Kim, Jaegwon (2005), *Physicalism, or Something Near Enough*. Princeton: Princeton University Press.

Kistler, Max (1998), Reducing Causality to Transmission, *Erkenntnis* 48, pp. 1–24.

Kistler, Max (1999/2006), *Causalité et lois de la nature*, Paris: Vrin, Collection Mathesis (1999), *Causation and Laws of Nature*, London: Routledge.

Kistler, Max (1999a), Causes as Events and Facts, *Dialectica* 53, pp. 25–46.

Kistler, Max (2006/2020), Lois, exceptions et dispositions, in Bruno Gnassounou and Max Kistler (eds.), *Les dispositions en philosophie et en sciences*, Paris: CNRS, 2006, pp. 175–194; translated by A. Morelli, Laws, Exceptions, and Dispositions, *The Journal for the Philosophy of Language, Mind and the Arts* 1, 2020, pp. 45–66.

Kistler, Max (2013), The Interventionist Account of Causation and Non-causal Association Laws, *Erkenntnis* 78, pp. 65–84.

Kistler, Max (2014), Analysing Causation in Light of Intuitions, Causal Statements, and Science, in Bridget Copley and Fabienne Martin (eds.), *Causation in Grammatical Structures*, Oxford: Oxford University Press, pp. 76–99.

Kistler, Max (2016), *L'esprit matériel: Réduction et émergence*. Paris: Editions d'Ithaque; 2d ed, Paris: Eliott, 2023; *The Material Mind. Emergence and Reduction*. BSPS Open Series. Calgary: Calgary University Press, forthcoming.

Kistler, Max (2017), Higher-Level, Downward and Specific Causation, in Michele Paolini Paoletti and Francesco Orilia (dir.), *Philosophical and Scientific Perspectives on Downward Causation*, New York: Routledge, pp. 54–75.

Kistler, Max (2021), Physics' Contribution to Causation, *Kriterion – Journal of Philosophy* 35, pp. 21–46.

Kistler, Max (2021a), Models of Downward Causation, in Jan Voosholz and Markus Gabriel (eds.), *Top-Down Causation and Emergence*. Cham: Springer, pp. 305–326.

Kitcher, Philip (1989), Explanatory Unification and the Causal Structure of the World, in Philip Kitcher and Wesley C. Salmon (eds.), *Minnesota Studies in the Philosophy of Science, Vol. XIII: Scientific Explanation*, Minneapolis: University of Minnesota Press, pp. 410–505.

Knobe, Joshua and B. Fraser (2008), Causal Judgment and Moral Judgment: Two Experiments, in W. Sinnott-Armstrong (ed.), *Moral Psychology, Volume 2: The Cognitive Science of Morality*, Cambridge, MA: MIT Press, pp. 441–447.

Konishi, Hiroyuki, Takayuki Okamoto, Yuichiro Hara, Okiru Komine, Hiromi Tamada, Mitsuyo Maeda, et al. (2020), Astrocytic Phagocytosis Is a Compensatory Mechanism for Microglial Dysfunction, *The EMBO Journal* 39, e104464.

Koslicki, Kathrin (2016), Where Grounding and Causation Part Ways: Comments on Schaffer, *Philosophical Studies* 173, pp. 101–112.

Kutach, Douglas (2014), *Causation*. Cambridge, UK: Polity Press.

Kvart, Igal (2001), Lewis's "Causation as Influence", *Australasian Journal of Philosophy* 79, pp. 409–421.

Lam, Vincent (2005), Causation and Space-Time, *History and Philosophy of the Life Sciences* 27, pp. 465–478.

Lange, Marc (2009), *Laws and Lawmakers: Science, Metaphysics and the Laws of Nature*, Oxford: Oxford University Press.

Lange, Marc (2016), *Because Without Cause: Non-Causal Explanations in Science and Mathematics*, Oxford: Oxford University Press.

Le Pore, Ernest, and Barry Loewer (1987), Mind Matters, *Journal of Philosophy* 84, pp. 630–642.

Lewis, David (1973a), *Counterfactuals*, Oxford: Blackwell.

Lewis, David (1973b/1986), Causation, in D. Lewis, *Philosophical Papers, Volume II*, New York: Oxford University Press, 1986, pp. 159–172.

Lewis, David (1979/1986), Counterfactual Dependence and Time's Arrow, in D. Lewis (ed.), *Philosophical Papers, Volume II*, New York: Oxford University Press, pp. 32–66.

Lewis, David (1983), New Work for a Theory of Universals. *Australasian Journal of Philosophy* 61, pp. 343–377.

Lewis, David (1986), Postscripts to 'Causation', in D. Lewis (ed.), *Philosophical Papers, Volume II*, New York: Oxford University Press, pp. 172–213.

Lewis, David (1986a), Events, in D. Lewis (ed.), *Philosophical Papers, vol. II*, New York: Oxford University Press, pp. 241–269.

Lewis, David (1986b), *On the Plurality of Worlds*, Oxford: Wiley-Blackwell.

Lewis, David (1994), Humean Supervenience Debugged, *Mind* 103, pp. 473–490.

Lewis, David (1994a), Reduction of Mind, in Guttenplan, S. (ed.), *A Companion to Philosophy of Mind*, Cambridge, MA: Blackwell, pp. 412–431.

Lewis, David (2000/2004), Causation as Influence, in Collins, John, Ned Hall, and L. A. Paul (eds.), *Causation and Counterfactuals*, Cambridge, MA: MIT Press, pp. 75–106.

Lewis, David (2004), Void and Object, in Collins, John, Ned Hall, and L. A. Paul (eds.), *Causation and Counterfactuals*, Cambridge, MA: MIT Press, pp. 277–290.

List, Christian and Peter Menzies (2009), Non-Reductive Physicalism and the Limits of the Exclusion Principle. *Journal of Philosophy* 106, pp. 475–502.

Lowe, E.J. (2000), Causal Closure Principles and Emergentism, *Philosophy* 75, pp. 571–585.

Mach, Ernst (1894), On the Principle of Comparison in Physics, in *Popular Scientific Lectures*. Trans. T. J. Cormack, 3rd ed., Chicago, Il: Open Court, 2012, pp. 236–258. eBook. www.gutenberg.org/files/39508/39508-h/39508-h.htm.

Mach, Ernst (1960), *The Science of Mechanics: A Critical and Historical Account of its Development*, trans. T. J. McCormack, 6th edn., LaSalle, Il: Open Court.

Machamer, Peter, Lindley Darden and Carl F. Craver (2000), Thinking about Mechanisms. *Philosophy of Science* 67, pp. 1–25.

Marshall, Dan, and Brian Weatherson (2023), Intrinsic vs. Extrinsic Properties, *The Stanford Encyclopedia of Philosophy* (Fall 2023 Edition), Edward N. Zalta & Uri Nodelman (eds.), https://plato.stanford.edu/archives/fall2023/entries/intrinsic-extrinsic/.

Maslen, Cei, Terry Horgan, Helen Daly (2009), Mental Causation, in Beebee, Helen, Christopher Hitchcock, and Peter Menzies (eds.) *The Oxford Handbook of Causation*, Oxford University Press, pp. 523–553.

Maudlin, Tim (2007), *The Metaphysics Within Physics*. Oxford: Clarendon Press.

Maudlin, Tim (2011), *Quantum Non-Locality and Relativity: Metaphysical Intimations of Modern Physics*, 3rd ed., Chichester: Wiley-Blackwell.

McDermott, Michael (1995), Redundant Causation, *The British Journal for the Philosophy of Science* 46, pp. 523–544.

McDonnell, Neil (2017), Causal Exclusion and the Limits of Proportionality, *Philosophical Studies* 174, pp. 1459–1474.

McKenzie, Kerry (2022), *Fundamentality and Grounding*, Cambridge, UK: Cambridge University Press.

McKitrick, Jennifer (2013), Review of S. Mumford and R. L. Anjum, Getting Causes from Powers, *Analysis* 73, pp. 402–404.

McLaughlin, Brian, and Karen Bennett (2018), Supervenience, *The Stanford Encyclopedia of Philosophy* (Winter 2023 Edition), Edward N. Zalta & Uri Nodelman (eds.), https://plato.stanford.edu/archives/win2023/entries/supervenience/.

Menzies, Peter (1996), Probabilistic Causation and the Pre-emption Problem, *Mind* 105, pp. 85–117.

Menzies, Peter (2009), Platitudes and Counterexamples, in Beebee, Helen, Christopher Hitchcock, and Peter Menzies (eds.), *The Oxford Handbook of Causation,* Oxford: Oxford University Press, pp. 341–367.

Menzies, Peter and Helen Beebee (2024), Counterfactual Theories of Causation, Edward N. Zalta and Uri Nodelman (eds.), *The Stanford Encyclopedia of Philosophy (Spring 2024 Edition)*, https://plato.stanford.edu/archives/spr2024/entries/causation-counterfactual/.

Menzies, Peter and Huw Price (1993), Causation as a Secondary Quality, *British Journal for the Philosophy of Science* 44, pp. 187–203.

Mills, Eugene (1996), Interactionism and Overdetermination, *American Philosophical Quarterly* 33, 105–117.

Molnar, George (2003), *Powers: A Study in Metaphysics*, Oxford: Oxford University Press.

Morange, Michel (2001), *The Misunderstood Gene*, Cambridge, MA: Harvard University Press.

Mumford, Stephen and Rani Lill Anjum (2010), A Powerful Theory of Causation, in Anna Marmodoro (ed.), *The Metaphysics of Powers: Their Grounding and Their Manifestation*, New York: Routledge, pp. 143–159.

Mumford, Stephen and Rani Lill Anjum (2011), *Getting Causes from Powers*, Oxford: Oxford University Press.

Nagel, Ernest (1961), *The Structure of Science*, London: Routledge and Kegan Paul.

Ney, Alyssa (2009), Physical Causation and Difference Making, *The British Journal for the Philosophy of Science* 60, pp. 737–764.

Ney, Alyssa (2012), Neo-positivist Metaphysics, *Philosophical Studies* 160, pp. 53–78.

Noordhof, Paul (2020), *A Variety of Causes*, Oxford: Oxford University Press.

Norton John D. (2003), Causation as Folk Science, *Philosophers' Imprint*, 3(4), 1–22, www.philosophersimprint.org/003004/; repr. in Huw Price and Richard Corry (eds.), *Causation, Physics, and the Constitution of Reality: Russell's Republic Revisited*, Oxford: Oxford University Press , pp. 11–44.

Norton, John D. (2007), Do the Causal Principles of Modern Physics Contradict Causal Anti-Fundamentalism? in Peter Machamer and Gereon Wolters (eds.), *Thinking about Causes. From Greek Philosophy to Modern Physics*, Pittsburgh: University of Pittsburgh Press, pp. 222–234.

Norton, John D. (2009). Is There an Independent Principle of Causality in Physics? *British Journal for the Philosophy of Science* 60, 475–86.

Orilia, Francesco and Michele Paolini Paoletti (2017), Three Grades of Downward Causation, in *Michele Paolini Paoletti and Francesco Orilia* (eds.), *Philosophical and Scientific Perspectives on Downward Causation*, New York: Routledge, pp. 25–41.

Papineau, David (2020), Naturalism, *The Stanford Encyclopedia of Philosophy* (Fall 2023 Edition), Edward N. Zalta & Uri Nodelman (eds.), https://plato.stanford.edu/archives/fall2023/entries/naturalism/.

Paul, L. A. (2009), Counterfactual Theories, Helen Beebee, Christopher Hitchcock, and Peter Menzies (eds.), *The Oxford Handbook of Causation*, Oxford: Oxford University Press, pp. 158–184.

Pearl, Judea (2000), *Causality. Models, Reasoning, and Inference*, Cambridge: Cambridge University Press.

Pearl, Judea, and Dana Mackenzie (2018), *The Book of Why: The New Science of Cause and Effect*, New York: Penguin Random House.

Popper Karl R. (1934), *Logik der Forschung*, 10th ed., Tübingen: J.C.B. Mohr, 1994, transl. by the author, with the assistance of Dr. Julius Freed and Lan Freed: *The Logic of Scientific Discovery*, London: Routledge.

Price, Huw (2001). Causation in the Special Sciences: The Case for Pragmatism. In M. C. Galavotti, P. Suppes, and D. Costantini (eds.), *Stochastic Causality.* Stanford, CA: CSLI Publications, pp. 103–121.

Price, Huw (2007), Causal Perspectivalism, in Huw Price and Richard Corry (eds.), *Causation, Physics, and the Constitution of Reality: Russell's Republic Revisited*, Oxford: Oxford University Press , pp. 250–292.

Price, Huw, and Brad Weslake (2009), The Time-Asymmetry of Causation, in Helen Beebee, Christopher Hitchcock, and Peter Menzies (eds.) *The Oxford Handbook of Causation*, Oxford: Oxford University Press, pp. 414–443.

Price, Huw and Richard Corry (eds.) (2007), *Causation, Physics, and the Constitution of Reality: Russell's Republic Revisited*, Oxford: Clarendon Press.

Psillos, Stathis (2004), A Glimpse of the Secret Connexion: Harmonizing Mechanisms with Counterfactuals. *Perspectives on Science* 12/3, pp. 288–319.

Psillos, Stathis (2009), Causal Pluralism, in Robrecht Vanderbeeken and Bart D'Hooghe (eds.) *Worldviews, Science and Us: Studies of Analytical Metaphysics: A Selection of Topics From a Methodological Perspective*, Ghent: World Scientific Publishers, pp. 131–151.

Quillien, Tadeg (2020), When do we think that X caused Y? *Cognition* 205: 104410.

Quine, Willard Van Orman (1973), *The Roots of Reference*. LaSalle, Il: Open Court.

Quine, Willard Van Orman (1985), Events and Reification, in LePore E. et McLaughlin B. (eds.), *Actions and Events: Perspectives on the Philosophy of Donald Davidson*, Oxford: Basil Blackwell.

Reichenbach, Hans (1928/1958), *Philosophie der Raum-Zeit-Lehre*. Repr. H.R., *Gesammelte Werke in 9 Bänden, Band 2*. Wiesbaden: Springer 1977. Engl. Transl. by Maria Reichenbach and John Freund, *The Philosophy of Space and Time*, New York: Dover, 1958.

Reichenbach, Hans (1951), *The Rise of Scientific Philosophy*, Berkeley: University of California Press.

Reichenbach, Hans (1956), *The Direction of Time*. New York: Dover.

Reid, Thomas (1788/2010), *Essays on the Active Powers of Man*, ed. Knud Haakonssen and James A. Harris. Edinburgh: Edinburgh University Press.

Reiss, Julian (2009), Causation in the Social Sciences: Evidence, Inference and Purpose. *Philosophy of the Social Sciences* 39, pp. 20–40.

Reutlinger, Alexander, and Juha Saatsi (eds.) (2018). *Explanation Beyond Causation. Philosophical Perspectives on Non-Causal Explanations*, Oxford: Oxford University Press.

Robb, David, John Heil and Sophie Gibb (2023), Mental Causation, in Edward N. Zalta and Uri Nodelman (eds.), *The Stanford Encyclopedia of Philosophy* (Spring 2023 Edition), https://plato.stanford.edu/archives/spr2023/entries/mental-causation/ .

Rodriguez-Pereyra, Gonzalo (2015), Grounding is not a Strict Order, *Journal of the American Philosophical Association* 1, pp. 517–534.

Ross, Don, and David Spurrett (2007), Notions of Cause: Russell's Thesis Revisited. *British Journal for the Philosophy of Science* 58, pp. 45–76.

Russell, Bertrand (1903), *The Principles of Mathematics*, Cambridge: Cambridge University Press.

Russell, Bertrand (1912/1919), On the Notion of Cause, in *Mysticism and Logic, and Other Essays*. London: Longmans, Green, pp. 180–208.

Russell, Bertrand (1948), *Human Knowledge: Its Scope and Limits*, London: Allan and Unwin, 5th edition, 1966.

Salmon, Wesley (1980), Probabilistic Causality, *Pacific Philosophical Quarterly* 61 (1-2), pp. 50–74.

Salmon, Wesley (1984), *Scientific Explanation and the Causal Structure of the World*, Princeton (New Jersey): Princeton University Press.

Salmon, Wesley (1994/1998), Causality Without Counterfactuals, *Philosophy of Science* 61, pp. 297–312; repr. in *Causality and Explanation*, New York: Oxford University Press, 1998, pp. 248–260.

Sartorio, Carolina (2020), More of a Cause? *Journal of Applied Philosophy* 37, pp. 346–363.

Schaffer, Jonathan (2000/2004), Trumping Preemption, in John Collins, Ned Hall, L.A. Paul (eds.), *Causation and Counterfactuals*, Cambridge, MA: MIT Press, pp. 59–73.

Schaffer, Jonathan (2000a), Causation by Disconnection, *Philosophy of Science* 67, pp. 285–300.

Schaffer, Jonathan (2005), Contrastive Causation, *Philosophical Review* 114, pp. 327–358.

Schaffer, Jonathan (2016), Grounding in the Image of Causation, *Philosophical Studies* 173, pp. 49–100.

Schaffner, Kenneth (1993), *Discovery and Explanation in Biology and Medicine*, Chicago, Il: University of Chicago Press.

Schrenk, Markus (2016), *Metaphysics of Science: A Systematic and Historical Introduction*, Oxford: Routledge.

Schurz, Gerhard (2002). *Ceteris paribus* Laws: Classification and Deconstruction, *Erkenntnis* 57, pp. 351–372.

Schurz, Gerhard (2017), Interactive Causes: Revising the Markov Condition, *Philosophy of Science* 84, pp. 456–479.

Shoemaker, Sydney (2007), *Physical Realization*, Oxford: Oxford University Press.

Sloman, Steven (2005), *Causal Models*. Oxford: Oxford University Press.

Sober, Elliott (2001), Venetian Sea Levels, British Bread Prices, and the Principle of the Common Cause, *The British Journal for the Philosophy of Science* 52, 331–346.

Spirtes, Peter, Clark Glymour, and Richard Scheines (2000), *Causation, Prediction, and Search*, Cambridge, MA: MIT Press.

Spirtes, Peter and Scheines, Richard (2004), Causal Inference of Ambiguous Manipulations, *Philosophy of Science* 71, pp. 833–845.

Sprenger, Jan (2018), Foundations of Probabilistic Theory of Causal Strength, *Philosophical Review* 127, pp. 371–398.

Strawson, Peter F. (1959), *Individuals. An Essay in Descriptive Metaphysics*, London: Methuen.

Suppes, Patrick (1970). *A Probabilistic Theory of Causality*, Amsterdam: North Holland.

Tahko, Tuomas E. (2021), *Unity of Science*, Cambridge: Cambridge University Press.

Thompson, Naomi (2018), Metaphysical Interdependence, Epistemic Coherentism, and Holistic Explanation, in Ricki Bliss and Graham Priest (eds.), *Reality and its Structure: Essays in Fundamentality*, New York: Oxford University Press, pp. 107–125.

Torretti, Roberto (1983), *Relativity and Geometry*, 2nd ed. New York: Dover.

Vaassen, Bram (2022), Halfway Proportionality, *Philosophical Studies* 179, pp. 2823–2843.

van Fraassen, Bas (1989), *Laws and Symmetry*, New York: Oxford University Press.

Vetter, Barbara (2015), *Potentiality: From Dispositions to Modality*, Oxford: Oxford University Press.

von Wright, Georg Henrik (1971), *Explanation and Understanding*, Ithaca, NY: Cornell University Press.

Wald, Robert M. (1984), *General Relativity*, Chicago: University of Chicago Press.

Waldmann, Michael R. (2017), *The Oxford Handbook of Causal Reasoning*, New York: Oxford University Press.

Weslake, Brad (forthcoming), Exclusion Excluded, in a volume edited by Alastair Wilson and Katie Robertson, Oxford University Press. http://bweslake.s3.amazonaws.com/research/papers/weslake_exclusion.pdf.

Williamson, Jon (2005), *Bayesian Nets and Causality: Philosophical and Computational Foundations*, Oxford: Oxford University Press.

Williamson, Jon (2009), Probabilistic Theories, in Helen Beebee, Christopher Hitchcock, and Peter Menzies (eds.) *The Oxford Handbook of Causation*, Oxford: Oxford University Press, pp. 185–212.

Wilson, Alastair (2018), Metaphysical Causation, *Nous* 52, pp. 723–751.

Wilson, Jessica M. (2011), Non-reductive Realization and the Powers-based Subset Strategy, *The Monist* 94, pp. 121–154.

Wilson, Jessica M. (2014), No Work for a Theory of Grounding, *Inquiry* 57, pp. 535–579.

Wilson, Jessica M. (2021), *Metaphysical Emergence*, Oxford: Oxford University Press.

Woodward, James (2003), *Making Things Happen: A Theory of Causal Explanation*, Oxford: Oxford University Press.

Woodward, James (2007), Causation with a Human Face, in Huw Price and Richard Corry (eds.), *Causation, Physics, and the Constitution of Reality: Russell's Republic Revisited*, Oxford: Oxford University Press , pp. 66–105.

Woodward, James (2008), Mental Causation and Neural Mechanisms, in Jakob Hohwy and Jesper Kallestrup (eds.), *Being Reduced: New Essays on*

Reduction, Explanation, and Causation, Oxford: Oxford University Press, pp. 218–262.

Woodward, James (2009), Agency and Interventionist Theories, in Helen Beebee, Christopher Hitchcock, and Peter Menzies (eds.) *The Oxford Handbook of Causation*, Oxford: Oxford University Press, pp. 234–262.

Woodward, James (2010), Causation in Biology: Stability, Specificity, and the Choice of Levels of Explanation, *Biology and Philosophy* 25, pp. 287–318.

Woodward, James (2011), Mechanisms Revisited. *Synthese* 183, pp. 409–427.

Woodward, James (2014), A Functional Account of Causation; or, A Defense of the Legitimacy of Causal Thinking by Reference to the Only Standard That Matters—Usefulness (as Opposed to Metaphysics or Agreement with Intuitive Judgment), *Philosophy of Science* 81, pp. 691–713.

Woodward, James (2015), Interventionism and Causal Exclusion, *Philosophy and Phenomenological Research* 91(2), pp. 303–347.

Woodward, James (2015a), Methodology, Ontology, and Interventionism, *Synthese* 192, pp. 3577–3599.

Woodward, James (2021), Downward Causation Defended, in Jan Voosholz and Markus Gabriel (eds.), *Top-Down Causation and Emergence*, Cham: Springer, pp. 217–251.

Woodward, James (2021a), *Causation with a Human Face, Normative Theory and Descriptive Psychology*, New York: Oxford University Press.

Wright, Sewall (1921), Correlation and Causation, *Journal of Agricultural Research* 20, pp. 557–585.

Wysocki, Tom (2023), The Underdeterministic Framework, *British Journal for the Philosophy of Science*. https://doi.org/10.1086/724450.

Yablo, Stephen (1992), Mental Causation, *Philosophical Review* 101, pp. 245–280.

Yang, Eric (2013), Eliminativism, Interventionism, and the Overdetermination Argument, *Philosophical Studies* 164, pp. 321–340.

Acknowledgments

Many people have helped me by providing me with critical comments on earlier versions of the manuscript. I would like to thank Thomas Blanchard, Toby Friend, Sam Kimpton-Nye, Etienne Ligout, Yanis Pianko, Tom Wysocki, and two anonymous referees for Cambridge Elements. Many thanks to the series editor Tuomas Tahko for his generous support. I have carried out the research for this Element during a partial research leave funded by Institut Universitaire de France.

Cambridge Elements

Metaphysics

Tuomas E. Tahko
University of Bristol

Tuomas E. Tahko is Professor of Metaphysics of Science at the University of Bristol, UK. Tahko specializes in contemporary analytic metaphysics, with an emphasis on methodological and epistemic issues: 'meta-metaphysics'. He also works at the interface of metaphysics and philosophy of science: 'metaphysics of science'. Tahko is the author of *Unity of Science* (Cambridge University Press, 2021, Elements in Philosophy of Science), *An Introduction to Metametaphysics* (Cambridge University Press, 2015) and editor of *Contemporary Aristotelian Metaphysics* (Cambridge University Press, 2012).

About the Series

This highly accessible series of Elements provides brief but comprehensive introductions to the most central topics in metaphysics. Many of the Elements also go into considerable depth, so the series will appeal to both students and academics. Some Elements bridge the gaps between metaphysics, philosophy of science, and epistemology.

Cambridge Elements ≡

Metaphysics

Elements in the Series

A full series listing is available at: www.cambridge.org/EMPH

Printed in the United States
by Baker & Taylor Publisher Services